ANN RADCLIFFE

ANN RADCLIFFE

A Bio-Bibliography

Deborah D. Rogers

Bio-Bibliographies in World Literature, *Number 4*

GREENWOOD PRESS
Westport, Connecticut • London

Library of Congress Cataloging-in-Publication Data

Rogers, Deborah D.
    Ann Radcliffe : a bio-bibliography / Deborah D. Rogers.
       p.   cm.—(Bio-bibliographies in world literature, ISSN
0894–2323 ; no. 4)
    Includes bibliographical references (p.) and index.
    ISBN 0–313–28379–6 (alk. paper)
    1. Radcliffe, Ann Ward, 1764–1823—Bibliography. 2. Gothic
revival (Literature)—Great Britain—Bibliography. 3. Women and
literature—England—Bibliography. 4. Horror tales, English—
Bibliography. I. Title. II. Series.
Z8730.335.R64 1996
[PR5204]
016.823'6—dc20   95–41982

British Library Cataloguing in Publication Data is available.

Library of Congress Catalog Card Number: 95–41982
ISBN: 0–313–28379–6
ISSN: 0894–2323

First published in 1996

Greenwood Press, 88 Post Road West, Westport, CT 06881
An imprint of Greenwood Publishing Group, Inc.

Printed in the United States of America

The paper used in this book complies with the
Permanent Paper Standard issued by the National
Information Standards Organization (Z39.48–1984).

10 9 8 7 6 5 4 3 2

To the memory of Myer Rogers

CONTENTS

PREFACE

The difficulties of writing about Ann Radcliffe's life are many. Since most of her important papers were not preserved, the biographer is forced to rely on Talfourd's 1826 Memoir of Radcliffe prefixed to *Gaston* (E131). This account, which was written from information supplied by Radcliffe's husband, is necessarily biased. The biography of Radcliffe in Chapter 1 goes beyond Talfourd's Memoir by including new material from the one substantial extant Radcliffe manuscript, her commonplace book in the Boston Public Library.

The organization of the primary and secondary bibliographies is chronological. The chapter on early reviews and notices ends in 1826 with the publication of Radcliffe's posthumous novel, *Gaston de Blondeville.* Where necessary, further details about the classification of sections are supplied in headnotes. Items in the secondary bibliography are prefixed by the alphanumerical codes indicated in the table of contents. Appendices include information about adaptations, abridgements, parodies, imitations, and spurious attributions.

ACKNOWLEDGMENTS

I am fortunate enough to have many debts to acknowledge. A University of Maine faculty summer research grant and a Women-in-the-Curriculum grant allowed me to complete this project. I owe additional thanks for support to Judith Bailey, Vice President for Research and Public Service, and to Leslie Flemming, Dean of the College of Arts and Humanities.

Antonia Forster generously gave me access to the forthcoming second volume of her important *Index to Book Reviews in England*. Thanks also go to Tristram Cole, Maryanne Yurchuk, Beth Simpson-Robie, Frank Campbell, Crystal Libby, Blossom Primer, William Bates, Adelaide P. Amore, Robert Hunting, Mary Anne Schofield, Doreen Alvarez Saar, Jane Crouch, Arline Sprague, and Patricia Srebrnik. I am especially grateful to Patrick Myers and Kristina Sigurdson.

The Lewis Walpole Library, Farmington, Connecticut, the Robert H. Taylor Collection of the Princeton University Library, and the Boston Public Library kindly allowed me to use their holdings. I would also like to acknowledge the University of Maine Library Reference and Interlibrary Loan staff, especially Mel Johnson, Christine Whittington, Libby Soifer, and Peggy Clark.

I owe additional thanks to my colleagues Harvey Kail, Virginia Nees-Hatlen, Burton Hatlen, Josephine Donovan, Cathleen and Paul Bauschatz, Laura Cowan, Ulrich Wicks, Tina and Bill Baker, Christina Stevens, Tina Passman, and Bill Small. As always, Marilyn Emerick has provided invaluable assistance.

The Greenwood Press editors have been a pleasure to work with. I especially appreciate the helpful suggestions of George Butler, Liz Leiba, and Barbara Zamat.

On a more personal note, I would like to acknowledge the University of Maine Children's Center, especially Barbara Turner and Kevin Duplissie. Marilyn, Marvin, Glenn, Michael, and Judy Rogers and Irene, Alex, and Robert Segal all provided support.

I am most thankful for the constant encouragement of my husband, Howard Paul Segal, who inspired this book. For bringing me all the joy that is a little boy, I am grateful to four of the best: my son, Rick, and my nephews, Jesse, Sam, and Matthew. I thank heaven for my new daughter, Raechel Maya, named in part after the gentle soul to whom I dedicate this book.

Deborah D. Rogers
Orono, Maine
January 29, 1995

CHRONOLOGY

1

THE LIFE OF ANN RADCLIFFE, 1764–1823

Two problems immediately confront anyone writing about Ann Radcliffe's life: the vexed genre of biography and the paucity of information about Radcliffe. In 1986 when my first book, a biography of the eighteenth-century bookseller John Almon, was published, I paid little attention to the ideology of genre (Rogers, *Bookseller*). Since that time, however, it has become impossible to approach biographical writing without a certain degree of self-consciousness. Biographical truth has come to be seen by many as inevitably elusive and flawed, biography as a genre, inherently voyeuristic and intrusive. Not only has the objectivity, neutrality, and fairness of the biographer been questioned, but the acknowledged biases of biographers are sometimes considered desirable. Arguing that the biographer necessarily influences the biography, many biographers insist on narrating from their own particular perspectives, as they view lives against the background of the particular historical and cultural circumstances that produced them.

It is, of course, impossible ever to write a "definitive" biography due to the power relationships between the biographer and the subject and the connected issues of intimacy, of personal involvement, of motivation, and of identification. Ultimately, we are unable to reconstruct completely what a life was really like since the difficulty is that of understanding another human being. Nevertheless, the desire to get at the truth about people has always been compelling.

Writing life stories of women, who, in many cases, were not taken seriously, invites further problems. Locating women's materials is often difficult since many of their important papers have disappeared, perhaps because they were considered too insignificant to preserve. Radcliffe's journals, letters, manuscripts, and other documents are, for the most part nonextant. The notable exceptions include a copy of the contract for *Udolpho* in the Sadleir-Black Collection, University of Virginia Library (reproduced in TC40),[1] and a note to a Miss Williamson in the Robert H. Taylor Collection, Princeton University Library.[2] I have relied considerably on the one substantial extant Radcliffe manuscript, a forty-two leaf commonplace book in the Chamberlain Collection, Boston Public Library (MS Ch.K.1.10; hereafter, BPL). To my knowledge, the only surviving portrait of Radcliffe is in the Bettman Archives. In addition, the Lewis Walpole Library has a letter from William Radcliffe to John Pinkerton, which I found useful for deciphering William's hand in Ann's BPL commonplace book.

That Christina Rossetti complained about the dearth of information concerning Radcliffe's life only sixty years after her death suggests that Radcliffe's papers disappeared almost immediately. This is especially frustrating because we know that Radcliffe kept journals. (For one thing, Talfourd excerpted her diary. See below.) Rossetti so admired Radcliffe that she attempted to write her biography but abandoned the effort due to the scarcity of materials. Responses to Rossetti's 1883 letter to the *Athenaeum* requesting information on Radcliffe were few (C60). On 29 June 1883, after describing the way she *"Radcliffized"* at the Museum, Rossetti lamented the lack of documentary evidence about Radcliffe, which eventually caused her to suspend her projected biography. Rossetti concluded that "the best resource is Talfourd after all, unless it be a *quotation* made by Walter Scott. I doubt if the Memoir is feasible . . . " (C60).

The Talfourd referred to by Rossetti is Sir Thomas Noon (Serjeant) Talfourd's 1826 Memoir of Radcliffe prefixed to *Gaston* (E131). The earliest full biography of Radcliffe, this account, which includes extracts from Radcliffe's journals, was written from information furnished by Radcliffe's husband. It forms the (necessarily biased) foundation of all subsequent biographies. The only other full-length biographies of Radcliffe are Aline Grant's undocumented and highly speculative 1951 account (F5) and Pierre Arnaud's 1976 psychobiography, which relates Radcliffe's works to her neuroses, speculating about her novels in terms of her repression and her sexual conflicts (F8).

In what follows, like Radcliffe's previous biographers, I am forced to rely on Talfourd. I will, however, also extensively analyze and quote new material from the manuscript of Radcliffe's commonplace book (BPL).

Arguably the most popular novelist of her day and the Mother of a female Gothic that has achieved almost mythical status, Ann Ward

Radcliffe was born in London on 9 July 1764, the only child of William
Ward and Ann Oates Ward, who was thirty-six years old at the time of
her daughter's birth. Although William Ward was a tradesman, the
owner of a haberdasher's shop at 19 Holborn in London, the family
was well connected. William Ward was close to his internationally famous uncle, William Cheselden, Surgeon to King George II. Ann Oates
descended from the respected De Witt family of Holland. Her cousin,
Sir Richard Jebb, was a fashionable London physician. Ann made frequent, extended visits to her maternal uncle-in-law, Thomas Bentley, of
the pottery firm Wedgwood and Bentley, at Chelsea, and, later, Turnham
Green, where she met many of the celebrities of the day. Widowed
(later remarried) and childless himself, Bentley was fond of children
and interested in their education.[3]

When Ann was seven or eight, the Wards gave up their haber-
dashery to move to Bath, where William Ward managed a branch of
Wedgwood and Bentley. Several loose insertions in the BPL commonplace book provide some evidence of the nature of Ann's relationship with her mother during this period. A letter from her mother
dated 15 August 1776, written when Ann was visiting the Stamfords
at Derby (her Uncle Bentley had by this time married into the Stam-
ford family), indicates that Ann's mother regarded her only child,
whom she addressed as "Nancy," with affection. Maintaining a didactic tone, she wishes her daughter "health and every enjoyment that
may contribute to the improvement of mind or person so as to make
you amiable or usefull in life. God Bless you my Dear child" (BPL).[4]
Almost exactly six years later, on 14 August 1782, Ann Oates Ward
detailed wishes to be carried out after her death. Exhibiting affection towards her husband and daughter, she is concerned about her
only child's moral rectitude and duty, urging her to remember that

> the only Road too Happyness is by Truth, & Virtue, &
> a strict adhearance too her Duty, in what ever Station
> of Life, she may be placed, & that it will be her Duty
> to promote her Fathers wellfair & Happyness as much
> as Lays in her power. I also hope he will treat her
> with Affection, & Kindness, for my Sake, who have
> don the utmost in my power; from the first of our
> union to promote his wellfair, & Happyness, in every
> Respect. (BPL)

That ill health probably prompted such a document may be indicated by a signed autograph note from Ann Ward to her daughter
dated 12 March 1783. Here Mrs. Ward complains, "I have been very
indifferent Lately with the Gout . . ." (BPL).

Brought up in and remaining faithful to the Established Church, Ann received a good, though not classical education, schooled, according to Talfourd, in "all womanly accomplishments" (E131 6). At Bath Ann met the Lee sisters and was greatly impressed by Sophia Lee's *The Recess* (1783-85).

In appearance, according to Talfourd, Radcliffe was beautiful, if short: "Mrs. Radcliffe was, in her youth, exquisitely proportioned, though she resembled her father, and his brother and sister, in being low of stature. Her complexion was beautiful, as was her whole countenance, especially her eyes, eyebrows, and mouth" (E131 105).

On 15 January 1787 at St. Michael's Church in Bath, Ann Ward married William Radcliffe, an Oxford graduate, who trained as a lawyer at the Inner Temple. After keeping several terms at one of the inns of court, he became editor and proprietor of a newspaper, *The English Chronicle.* The young couple moved to London, where William had been born and raised.

The Radcliffes had no children. Although childbirth dominated women's culture, the biological dangers of pregnancy in an era before the introduction of antiseptic procedures and the medicalization of childbirth may have persuaded many women who were serious about writing to remain childless, if not single (Rogers, "Childbirth"). Virginia Woolf found it "significant that of the four great women novelists—Jane Austen, Emily Brontë, Charlotte Brontë, and George Eliot—not one had a child, and two were unmarried" (45). To this list of childless women authors, one could add not only Woolf herself, but also many earlier female writers, including Margaret Cavendish, Mary Astell, Aphra Behn, Clara Reeve, and Ann Radcliffe. It is hardly surprising that few children populate Radcliffe's novels.

Talfourd describes Radcliffe as so domestic that she was "minutely attentive to her household affairs," keeping exact records of every disbursement until shortly before her death (E131 98-99). Her leisure hours were spent reading, singing, and attending operas, oratorios, and plays. At the theater, the Radcliffes would sit in the pit, partly to avoid attracting attention (E131 100).

According to Talfourd, Radcliffe was formal and reserved, if not "old fashioned": "She felt . . . a distaste to the increasing familiarity of modern manners, to which she had been unaccustomed in her youth; and, though remarkably free and cheerful with her relatives and intimate friends, she preferred the more formal politeness of the old school among strangers" (E131 13).

By all accounts, Radcliffe led an uneventful, retired life. According to Talfourd,

> In drawing aside the veil from the personal course of
> this celebrated lady, her biographer cannot exhibit
> any of the amusing varieties, which usually chequer
> the lives of successful authors: here are no brilliant
> conversational triumphs; no elaborate correspon-
> dence with the celebrated, or the great; no elegant
> malice; no anecdotes of patrons or rivals; none of
> fashion's idle pastime, nor of controversy's more idle
> business. Even the great events of Mrs. Radcliffe's
> life, the successive appearances of her novels, extend
> over a small part only of its duration. (E131 4)

Later in the nineteenth century, J. Cordy Jeaffreson patronizingly
generalized to find such lack of activity typical of women authors:
"Like many, and perhaps we may add *the best* of our female writers,
Mrs. Radcliffe passed a retired life . . ." (F20 No. 70).

Radcliffe's seclusion came in for special attention in *The Edinburgh
Review*: "[N]othing was known of her but her name in the title page.
She never appeared in public, nor mingled in private society, but
kept herself apart, like the sweet bird that sings its solitary notes,
shrowded and unseen" (E122 360n).

Radcliffe's insistence on privacy relates to her excessive shyness.
Talfourd attributes much of Radcliffe's diffidence to her attitude
towards authorship: "There was . . . in the feeling of old gentility,
which most of her relatives cherished, a natural repugnance to authorship, which she never entirely lost . . ." (E131 6-7). Perhaps
internalizing such notions, Radcliffe was unlike such earlier self-
confident female writers as Aphra Behn or Margaret Cavendish (respectively considered promiscuous and mad because of their immod-
esty). Like Fanny Burney, Radcliffe was reticent about authorship.
Her delicacy, however, failed to prevent contemporaries from think-
ing she was insane. (See below.)

In the frame of one of her best works, *The Italian*, Radcliffe
adopts a male narrative voice—that of the proverbial "student of
Padua"—to apologize for her writing: "You will perceive from the
work, that this student was very young, as to the arts of
composition . . ." (4). While such disclaimers are partially due to
convention, considered with her extreme shyness and withdrawal
from society, such self-deprecation may indicate feelings of inadequacy.

Ironically, Radcliffe's very success may have later encouraged her
shyness. According to *The New Monthly Magazine*, "The splendour of
her own reputation alarmed her feminine apprehensiveness and

pride, and she shrunk from it into entire seclusion" (F20 No. 43).
Talfourd represents Radcliffe as diffident and withdrawn, even at
her most popular:

> The reputation, which Mrs. Radcliffe derived from
> her writings did not draw her from the retirement, in
> which they were written. . . . She would, indeed, have
> conferred honour and obligation on any circle, which
> she could prevail on herself to join; but a scrupulous
> self-respect, almost too nice to be appreciated in these
> days, induced her sedulously to avoid the appear-
> ance of reception, on account of her literary fame.
> The very thought of appearing in person as the au-
> thor of her romances shocked the delicacy of her
> mind. To the publication of her works she was con-
> strained by the force of her own genius; but nothing
> could tempt her to publish *herself*, or to sink for a
> moment, the gentlewoman in the novelist. (E131 12-
> 13)

The Literary Gazette was (unfortunately) unique in its horrified
reaction to Radcliffe's attitude towards female authorship:

> She was ashamed, (*yes, ashamed*) of her own talents;
> and was ready to sink in the earth at the bare suspi-
> cion of any one taking her for an author; her chief
> ambition being to be thought a lady! . . . It is a sad
> balk to the mind to imagine this extraordinary au-
> thoress, during the creation of her works, suddenly
> alarmed by a knock at the door, and hiding her ad-
> mired pages, as if they were the spoils of theft, that
> nothing might interfere with her appearance as a
> gentlewoman, according to the most established rules.
> To belong to the glorious assembly dignified by the
> names of Homer, Virgil, Dante, Shakespeare, Ariosto,
> Tasso, Spencer, and Milton, is nothing: but to be
> equal to one's neighbours in the estimation of a com-
> mittee of old women of quality, and, above all, not to
> be suspected of authorship, is the very summit of
> human felicity. (F20 No. 42)

More characteristic in the nineteenth century was admiration of
Radcliffe's female diffidence. For example, Richard Henry Dana
found, "There is a beauty in her mind, a gentleness, a delicacy, a

retiredness in her disposition, which is wholly feminine, and which every man cannot but feel, who feels as man ought towards woman; a disposition, which she who wants, though she may draw admiration, will never win and hold a true, respectful, knightly sentiment of love" (F20 44). Richard Garnett praised Radcliffe's diffidence in terms of the general attitude of female writers, paying tribute to the "sensitive aversion to notice which she shared with many other authoresses" (F20 No. 77). Such impressions may indicate a lack of self-esteem on the part of women writers as a whole.

It was not until after her marriage at the age of twenty-three that Radcliffe began writing. Talfourd (from information supplied by William Radcliffe, who may be self-serving) begins the tradition of crediting William with encouraging his shy, insecure wife to write: "[I]t does not seem, that the peculiar bent of her genius was perceived till after her marriage. . . . Encouraged by him [William], she soon began to employ her leisure in writing; and, as her distrust of herself yielded to conscious success, proceeded with great rapidity" (E131 6-7). Talfourd also begins the condescending tradition that Radcliffe wrote merely to wile away the evening hours, when her husband was working:

> Mr. Radcliffe, about this time, became proprietor of "The English Chronicle," and took an active share in the management of the paper, which, with other avocations, obliged him to be frequently absent from home till a late hour in the evening. On these occasions, Mrs. Radcliffe usually beguiled the else weary hours by her pen. . . . (E131 7-8)

Influenced by Talfourd (or, more accurately, perhaps, by William Radcliffe), later critics, with Dorothy Scarborough, fail to take Radcliffe seriously, attributing her literary endeavors to the fact that ". . . she had time that was wasting on her hands . . . " (T17 16). Similarly, according to Aline Grant, who echoes Talfourd's language, "Waiting for William's return in these long evening hours, with all her household duties done and complete freedom from interruption assured, Ann began beguiling the time with putting down on paper some of the romantic scenes on which her imagination loved to dwell . . ." (F5 46).

Six of Radcliffe's works appeared in her lifetime, with amazing speed in the eight years from 1789 to 1797. (A seventh was published posthumously.) Starting with *The Castles of Athlin and Dunbayne*, which appeared when she was only twenty-five years old, Radcliffe anonymously published her first three novels in three years.

Published in 1789, Radcliffe's anonymous first performance, *The Castles of Athlin and Dunbayne*, received little notice. Perfunctorily commending the novel for its moral sentiments, early reviews were unenthusiastic if not patronizing. For example, the negative review in *The Monthly Review* praises the morality, even as it implicitly proclaims that the work will appeal only to women and children, to "the young and unformed mind. To men who have passed, or even attained, the meridian of life, a series of events, which seem not to have their foundation in nature, will ever be insipid, if not disgustful" (F20 No. 2).

Here begins the focus on morality and the patronizing tradition of considering Radcliffe's works as childish. For example, in 1805 Hugh Murray found that Radcliffe's scenes of terror afforded undeniable pleasure that "till her time, was confined chiefly to the nursery" (F20 No. 49). Such remarks must have pained Radcliffe. Given her diffident and insecure nature, it is surprising that these attacks failed to inhibit her writing.

Radcliffe's debut was also greeted by criticism of historical inaccuracies that would continue to plague her. In this case *The Critical Review* took the author of *Athlin and Dunbayne* (assumed to be male) to task for the inauthentic rendering of the Highlands (F20 No. 1).

Later critics seldom pay attention to *Athlin and Dunbayne.* Radcliffe's first experiment is generally considered unremarkable.

Only one year after *Athlin and Dunbayne* was published, Radcliffe's second novel, *A Sicilian Romance*, appeared anonymously. This attempt likewise received relatively little attention. Contemporaries praised this novel for its decorum, morality, originality, and elegant language, despite its improbabilities. Later critics seldom study this novel except for primarily historical purposes.

If *Athlin and Dunbayne* and *Sicilian Romance* are generally considered experimental, Radcliffe's reputation rests primarily on her next three novels, *The Romance of the Forest* (1791), *The Mysteries of Udolpho* (1794), and *The Italian* (1797). These are universally thought to be her best works.

Published the year after *A Sicilian Romance,* Radcliffe's *Romance of the Forest* was met with rave reviews. With the publication of this Gothic, the anonymous female author (*Romance of the Forest* was "By the Authoress of A Sicilian Romance") became one of the most popular novelists of the day. The success of this novel may have encouraged the reticent Radcliffe, who had not previously acknowledged any of her work, to acknowledge the second edition of *The*

Romance of the Forest when it appeared in 1792. It was *The Romance of the Forest* that established Radcliffe's reputation. This novel first displayed the full power of her poetic descriptions, demonstrating, as Sir Walter Scott put it, that she had "the eye of a painter, with the spirit of a poet" (F20 No. 59). His assessment has been echoed repeatedly through the years. If Radcliffe's first two novels are mediocre, she comes of age with *The Romance of the Forest.* Even so, today *The Romance of the Forest* is virtually ignored—despite its contemporary status and popularity.

The Romance of the Forest may have established Radcliffe's reputation, but it was *Udolpho* that catapulted her to fame. Although *Udolpho* was all the rage with the public, the immediate response in journals was decidedly mixed. They praised the novel for its hallmark and pioneering poetical descriptions of landscapes and creation of suspense but criticized the interspersed verses, anachronisms, improbabilities, excessive descriptions, inadequate characterization, and explained supernatural. That such criticisms resurface in the reception of Radcliffe's later work and in general considerations of her place in literary history is perhaps unfair: Radcliffe seems to have paid attention to reviews, improving as a result in *The Italian.*

Recently *Udolpho* and Radcliffe's other novels have been approached with new seriousness and appreciation. One of the most important current directions in Radcliffe criticism is the analysis of Radcliffe's heroines in their role as women and in their relationships with their mothers. Feminist critics have recently observed that although the Gothic novel has traditionally been seen to reflect patriarchal violence, starting with Ann Radcliffe, the "female Gothic" has also emphasized female kinship relations, especially the mother-daughter bond in terms of the mother's threat to engulf her child and the daughter's issues of separation. At the dramatic heart of the Radcliffean Gothic is the daughter's conflict with maternal figures from whom she cannot totally separate because of her own femaleness and because they symbolize her own fate if she, too, becomes a mother.

After the publication of *Udolpho*, in the summer of 1794, Radcliffe went traveling with her husband. This trip to Holland (the home of the De Witts, her maternal ancestors), western Germany, and the Rhine represented the only time she ever went abroad, although her vivid descriptions of countries like southern France and Italy, which she never visited, would seem to argue otherwise. After returning from the Continent, the Radcliffes toured the English Lake District. The following year Radcliffe published an account of this excursion, *A Journey Made in the Summer of 1794.* . . . If early reviewers found the

Journey less exciting than Radcliffe's novels, it was generally praised for its reflections and descriptions. Even so, the *Journey* is discussed little today except in terms of Radcliffe's other works.

Joseph Farington's diary provides a description of the Radcliffes during these years. Mistaking William Ward's occupation, as well as Ann's age, which must have been thirty-three at the time, he relays some of Giuseppe Marchi's personal observations about the couple, who, by this time, had moved to St. George's Fields, Southwark:

> Marchi called—He dined yesterday with Mr & Mrs Radcliffe the Authoress—She is daughter to Mr Ward who was a Bookseller at Bath. Mrs Radcliffe is 27 or 8 years old, a pretty face. Marchi told her of Johnson & Goldsmith coming to Sir Joshua Reynolds, she said, those were fine times. Mr Radcliffe was educated at Oxford—He is now Editor of an Evening paper, for which He paid £1000—He is abt. 30 years old and democratically inclined. They reside at No. 7 Medina Place—St. Georges fields. (E43)

In another of the few surviving contemporary descriptions of Radcliffe, Charles Bucke characterizes her at a dinner party at her house:

> Her conversation was delightful! She sung *Adeste Fideles* with a voice mellow and melodious, but somewhat tremulous. Her countenance indicated melancholy. She had been, doubtless, in her youth, beautiful. She was a great admirer of Schiller's Robbers. Her favourite tragedy was Macbeth. Her favourite painters were, Salvator, Claude, and Gasper Poussin; her favourite poets, after Shakespeare, Tasso, Spenser, and Milton. (F20 No. 61)

After her first and only excursion abroad, Ann traveled, once or twice a year, within England with her husband. Radcliffe kept a private diary of these journeys, later excerpted and included in Talfourd's Memoir. (The original diary does not appear to have survived.) In the fall of 1797, the Radcliffes visited the coast of Kent. The same year saw the publication of Radcliffe's next novel, *The Italian.*

As noted, Radcliffe appears to have taken the criticism of her novels, especially *Udolpho*, to heart. Set in the present, *The Italian*

(1797) contains no anachronisms. The explained supernatural is less vociferous and the landscape descriptions more succinct. Gone are the interspersed verses. Characterization also improved with the creation of Schedoni. For these reasons, from the start, *The Italian* has been regarded as an improvement on Radcliffe's previous romances, even if some personally prefer earlier works. In 1900 Andrew Lang called *The Italian* the "roof and crown of Mrs. Radcliffe's work" (F20 No. 80). Many would agree.

From the beginning, *The Italian* invited comparisons with Reeve and Walpole. As might be expected, since *Udolpho* (1794) inspired *The Monk* (1795), which in turn, inspired a reaction in the form of *The Italian* (1797), Lewis, with his unexplained supernatural, has often been compared to Radcliffe, with her explained mysteries.

Radcliffe's heroine in *The Italian* comes in for relatively little discussion. Perhaps this is because, as Kate Ellis observes, while *Udolpho* is Radcliffe's most female-centered novel, *The Italian* is Radcliffe's least female-centered novel insofar as its focus is on the developing consciousness of the villain rather than the heroine (TC231). It is interesting in this respect that such a novel should often be regarded as Radcliffe's best work. Perhaps Radcliffe invested herself too much in her women characters and needed a male-centered novel to explore fully the dark side of the unconscious. The character of the villain may have provided her with the intellectual and emotional distance she was unable to attain with her female characters. Nevertheless, much as they did with *Udolpho*, modern critics are beginning to focus on the female relationships in *The Italian*.

Shortly after the publication of *The Italian*, on 24 July 1798, Ann's father, William Ward, died, leaving his only child with interests in the rents of property in Houghton-on-the-Hill, near Leicester. To Mrs. Ward went their house in Bath and the right to raise money on their house in Leicester. William Radcliffe was also provided for in the event that he should outlive Ann (F5 91). Perhaps as a diversion from the grief caused by her father's death, some two months later, in September of 1798, Ann set out with William for Portsmouth, the Isle of Wight, and Winchester.

In the spring of 1799 William Radcliffe was apparently ill, causing Ann to decline the offer of Elizabeth Carter, the famous scholar, to visit her (E131 94). Around this time the Radcliffes gave up the house in St. George's Fields and took a house a short distance to the southwest of it in China Terrace, Lambeth (F5 97).

Two years after William Ward's death, Ann Oates Ward died, leaving most of her property to her daughter with the provision that nothing be left to William and that none of the bequest be used to pay off William's debts (F5 98). Ann's inheritance, together with the considerable profits from her novels, left her in comfortable circumstances. At least by this time, she did not need to publish to generate income. Indeed, she published no more novels during her lifetime. For several years after the death of her parents, Radcliffe wrote nothing of major significance, spending most of her time secluded at home or traveling around England.

Perhaps again to escape feelings of grief, the Radcliffes, in the summer of 1800, following Ann Ward's death, toured the southern coast of England, taking along Chance, Ann's favorite dog (E131 41). For an only child to have lost both father and mother in such a relatively short span must have been devastating. In her private journal of the trip, Radcliffe poignantly expressed her sense of loss, if not abandonment, and her state of solitary being: "In this month, on the 24th of July, my dear father died two years since: on the 14th of last March, my poor mother followed him: I am the last leaf on the tree!" (E131 39)

That fall the Radcliffes spent two weeks at Little Hampton. In autumn of the following year (1801), they traveled to Southampton and Lymington and returned to the Isle of Wight. The next fall (1802) found the Radcliffes visiting Leicester, Warwick, Woodstock, and Oxford, taking in such attractions as Warwick Castle, Blenheim, and Kenilworth Castle.

It was Kenilworth Castle that inspired *Gaston de Blondeville*, written in the winter of 1802 and published posthumously. Although this was Radcliffe's last novel, she continued to write some poetry.

Perhaps in reaction to criticism of her explained mysteries, Radcliffe, in *Gaston* offers no explanations for the supernatural. Reviewers, however, found Radcliffe's specter troubling, condemning it as "a daylight sort of ghost" (F20 No. 44), a "flat-footed apparition" that "alarms far less than the tiniest mouse scurrying in the wainscot of Udolpho" (F20 No. 89). It is not altogether surprising that today Radcliffe's last work is almost totally ignored.

Several years after she wrote *Gaston*, in June, 1805, Mrs. Radcliffe visited Lord Eardley's mansion, Belvedere House, and in the fall of 1807, the Radcliffes visited Knole House. Apparently four years elapsed before Mrs. Radcliffe journeyed out again, returning to Portsmouth and the Isle of Wight and visiting Penshurst, the seat of the Sydneys, and Malvern. Several years later, around 1815, the Radcliffes moved to what would be Ann's last home, 5 Stafford Row in Pimlico (F5 137).

During this time, Radcliffe stopped writing for publication. Although her previous novel, *The Italian,* had been published to great acclaim in 1797, Radcliffe declined to publish *Gaston* during her lifetime. In the twenty-six years from the publication of *The Italian* until Radcliffe's death in 1823, mysteriously, she published no new romances. In fact, she virtually stopped publishing at the age of thirty-four, after achieving her greatest success. Many assumed that Radcliffe had died or gone insane (E131 4). Sir Walter Scott admits that for a time he, himself, believed rumors that "in consequence of brooding over the terrors which she depicted, her reason had at length been overturned, and that the author of *The Mysteries of Udolpho* only existed as the melancholy inmate of a private mad-house" (F20 No. 59). In the total absence of documentation, contemporaries were willing to believe, presumably because she was the reserved (female) author of Gothics, that Radcliffe was insane. Such interpretations are common problems in constructing a woman's life without proper evidence.

So reticent and self-effacing was Radcliffe that she never corrected rumors of her death or madness. Julia Kavanagh remarked, "She who could allow herself to be proclaimed dead or insane and not remonstrate, was no ordinary woman" (F20 No. 71).

In 1837 Charles Bucke refuted charges of Radcliffe's insanity: "There was, for many years, a report that this accomplished lady was inflicted with insanity. How the report came to be raised I know not; but, I believe, it never was the case. She had not only an elegant taste, but a comprehensive understanding" (F20 No. 61).

If Radcliffe was not mad, why did she stop publishing? According to Talfourd, after *The Italian*, Radcliffe "declined again to subject herself to criticism by publication" (E131 89). Radcliffe must have derived pleasure from appreciations of her work by some of her most famous contemporaries. Criticism, however, undoubtedly offended and dismayed the insecure author.

Talfourd also indicates that after Radcliffe no longer needed the money, she lost some of her incentive to write: "At first the sums she received, though not necessary, were welcome; but, as her pecuniary resources became more ample, she was without sufficient excitement to begin on an extended romance . . ." (E131 89-90). Another reason Radcliffe stopped publishing after *The Italian* and stopped writing fiction altogether after *Gaston* may have been the parodies as well as the many inferior imitations of her work.

During her last twelve years, Radcliffe apparently suffered respiratory problems, which may at times have left her too debilitated to write. According to Sir Charles Scudamore, M.D., the physician who attended her during her last year, "Mrs. Radcliffe had been for several years subject to severe catarrhal coughs, and also was occasionally afflicted with asthma" (E131 103).

In any account of her illness, Radcliffe's commonplace book (BPL) is of considerable importance. Unfortunately, this manuscript, which is in deteriorating condition, has been largely ignored. The only previous biographer to cite it is Arnaud, who translates several passages into French (F8). The commonplace book provides a detailed account of Radcliffe's health and her personal concerns during her last year of life. Since Radcliffe's published journals (*Journey Made in the Summer of 1794* and Talfourd's extracts) consist, for the most part, of impersonal descriptions, the commonplace book affords us a rare glimpse of Radcliffe's private thoughts.[5]

According to Talfourd, who, of course, was influenced by William Radcliffe, Ann's husband cared for her with "unwearied attentions." In this instance, William's devotion to Ann—at least during this period—is confirmed by the commonplace book, where many of Radcliffe's prescriptions appear to have been painstakingly copied, almost certainly, by her husband. His concern about the accuracy of his transcriptions attests to his anxiety regarding his wife's treatment. (See, for example, BPL 1 June 1822.)

According to Scudamore, Radcliffe experienced respiratory problems in March, 1822, but improved in the summer: "In March 1822, she was ill with inflammation of the lungs, and for a considerable time remained much indisposed. With the summer season and change of air, she regained a tolerable state of health" (E131 103).

By summer, Scudamore must mean the period from around 12 June 1822 to the end of August (with the exception of an attack July 24 to 26) because, according to her commonplace book, Radcliffe was quite ill throughout May and the beginning of June, 1822. During this period, she changed health-care providers several times. On May 17th, 18th, and 23rd, a Mr. Ollier treated her for severe asthmatic spasms. Perhaps a sense of decorum prevented Talfourd and Scudamore from mentioning that Radcliffe also experienced intestinal complaints. Dr. Garthshore prescribed medication for stomach and bowel problems. Although such discomfort is not indicated in the journal up to this point, Mr. Ollier's first prescription (which had included Sulphatis Magnesiae or Epsom salts, known for cathartic properties) provides some evidence that constipation had previously accompanied Radcliffe's asthma. (It is, of course, entirely possible that Radcliffe's various medications themselves contributed to intestinal difficulties.)

Along with stomach ailments, Radcliffe's respiratory problems continued. She found "considerable relief" from Dr. Berkeley's prescription for a Mrs. Norris for "a cough with hard breathing." The medication "causes perspiration and eases the breathing."

By the end of May, Radcliffe was seeing Scudamore. Because he prescribed the rest of the medications in her notebook and attended her during her last illness, it appears that he remained her physician for the rest of her life, short as this period was.

On May 28 and 30 and on June 1, 3, and 6, Scudamore prescribed medication to relieve respiratory problems. Since some of his prescriptions contain ingredients such as Liqu. Calcis, which was used for dyspepsia and diarrhea, Radcliffe's stomach problems presumably failed to abate. Indeed, on June 12, Scudamore wrote a prescription specifically for intestinal complaints. During this time, Radcliffe sought comfort from tea: "I have generally *always* found *some* relief from warm tea, especially if I could eat a little."

At least during this period, Radcliffe's suffering must have been acute, rendering her, at times, too ill or uncomfortable to write or to socialize. Or she may have been too sedated: some of Scudamore's prescriptions contain ingredients such as Connii (hemlock), papau (syrup of poppy), or Opii (opium) that have soporific or narcotic effects.

Radcliffe may have been feeling better between June 12 and July 23, as more than a month elapsed between her prescriptions. On July 23, however, Radcliffe experienced a mild spasm, but felt well enough to make a trip to see Dr. Scudamore: "I had been much better for the last prescriptions but had this morning early a spasm. After breakfast I was so much better that I went to Doc S."

Her condition deteriorated rapidly: "In going through the Park however I became worse, but reached a coach in St. James street. When we reached Dr. S. I was almost speechless. Waited half an hour and little better when I saw him. He said I ought not to have come out."

Scudamore judged her condition serious enough to require bloodletting and applying a blister: "Ordered immediate bleeding and blistering, with the 7th Prescriptions. Said he wd call tomorrow. I reached home wth great difficulty."

Radcliffe discreetly omitted the name of the person who bled her: "Was soon bled by Mr. [blank] (Strand). Fainted and remained long helpless tho not senseless. Very weak all day; applied a blister to the stomach. My breathing relieved by bleeding before the blister rose."

Radcliffe was better the next day, when Scudamore requested a urine sample:

> The next day felt so light and well that I ran down
> stairs. Doc[r] Scudamore called; examined the blood with

> a spoon. (it looked dark and heavy, and M[r] [blank]
> had said it was very necessary to lose such.) Doc[r] S. said
> nothing; but desired some water, of night and morn-
> ing, might be saved, and he would call the day after the
> morrow. He left the eight prescriptions. He seemed to
> have some new view of my case, and asked particularly
> if I had had any pains on the right side. No. He pressed
> gently my sides and repeated the question; still no. If I
> had ever pains or stitch in the shoulder blade. I recol-
> lected that on the drawing-room day, when I had fainted
> in the G Park, after standing some hours, tho not in a
> crowd, the fit was preeceded by cold shivering and
> sharp pains about the right shoulder blade, which
> seemed to cause the fainting. Advised me to remain at
> home and quiet.

Since Scudamore's prescriptions merely increased the dosages of the
same medications he had already been prescribing, his ostensibly
"new view" of the case must not have differed dramatically from his
initial opinion.

With the exception of this brief incident in July, Radcliffe seems
to have felt better from around June 12 to November 12. On July
26th, Radcliffe, much improved, saw Scudamore for the last time
until November, after she returned from a trip to Ramsgate:

> July 26 Surprizingly better; no spasm or difficulty of
> breathing. Had an airing yesterday with benefit. Doc[r]
> S. called. examined the water, pale and clear, that at
> night had at first some cloud in the centre, which
> afterwards settled. Pale and clear for some time
> [past?] usually; but sometimes very thick and reddish
> and scanty. Doc[r] S. on going away, said the the [re-
> peated in the MS] liver was affected—slightly affected.
> He had once before expressed a doubt of this, when
> I drew my hand athwart my stomach to describe where
> the tightness of the spasm most affected me, and had
> asked me the same questions he had done on the
> 24th. He said I was much better, and he hoped he
> should soon make me well. Desired to see me in a
> few days.

Radcliffe wrote that she had been feeling better from July 26, the
last time she saw Scudamore, until September 24th:

> He [Scudamore] wrote the ninth prescriptions, which I
> have taken regularly, till the beginning of Septr. when I
> nearly left off the pills once [word unreadable] a week
> and took the mixture irregularly, sometimes only once
> a day or omitting it for two or three days, on which days
> I seemed not so easy athwart the stomach and more
> [word unreadable] I have had no spasm or difficulty of
> breathing, even in the early morning since I was bled,
> and have taken the 9th prescription. I have been so well,
> that I have not thought it necessary to see Doc. Scud,
> since the 26 of July and now on the 24th of Sept. on
> enquiring find that he has left town, and that I must
> take our journey without consulting him. I have had
> frequent airings with little walks since the 14th of June,
> air and exercise without fatigue and perspiration. This
> week we have concluded wth the carriage. I have not quite
> lost the parched mouth on waking, or the feverish
> bed. . . .

Radcliffe's concerns about her digestion (which she refers to as often as her respiratory condition) indicate that she continued to suffer
stomach problems, which, however, by this time seem minor. The wild
rumors that circulated about Radcliffe included speculations that she
chose her food to encourage nightmares: "[F]or the purpose of filling
her sleep with those phantoms of horror . . . [Radcliffe] is said to have
supped upon the most indigestible substances . . . " (C5 57). Despite
such gossip, Radcliffe's diet appears to have been conservative, allowing
at most a little porter, or dark brown beer:

> During this time (fr July to latter end of Sept^r.) my diet
> has been chocolate (Stan Sloan's) for breakfast and one
> dish tea. for dinner a little meat, some puddings, rice,
> crust of bread or biscuit after tea. A very little porter,
> now and then; half a glass of sherry mint wth water after
> dinner, and grapes, toast of water at dinner and not half
> a pint of that or any hardly after two dishes of tea. I am
> convinced that but little liquid is best for my digestion.

In the beginning of October, Radcliffe was well enough to travel to Ramsgate. Although fog exacerbated her respiratory condition, and her dietary concerns persisted, she began to feel stronger:

> On the 3d of Octr. we set off for Dover and Ramsgate, without having seen Dr. S. since the 26 of July. The uneasiness I had for some time felt about the right kidney was much relieved after the 2d day's jumble, which seemed to occasion the very thick water made for some days after, so I know the remedy for that pain, for I had no return of it all the while I was fr home, nor soon after my return; nor any spasm or difficulty of breathing except on some foggy mornings at R. and at home. I walked a great deal there and well and grew stronger and in better spirits. I was on the Pier-head for hours. [word unreadable] in very high winds and bore it well. Walked 5 miles to Broad-stairs and back, hardly sitting down, but was much fatigued for [want?] of resting. Still I had a parched mouth, and was restless in the nights, tho' I never took supper and hardly tasted wine, and [mint?] wth water. But we had often seasoned dishes, and I had about half a pint of thin table-ale at dinner, drinking some water (very soft and pleasant, after, and eating pears.[)] Swanseggs. I continued to take occasionally the pills and mixture of the last prescription, the 9th and found the inward fever kept down particularly by the mixture. Sometimes took Miss Wilson's pills On the whole I have returned much strengthened and better, and continue daily exercise in the park. I have found my breathing lately affected by the fog and the north wind.
> Nov. 12. We were absent 4 weeks.

It is possible that Radcliffe's health improved because she was taking less medication. Her restlessness at night may, however, indicate some degree of withdrawal.

Because Radcliffe's ailments, asthma and indigestion, often have psychological components, it is tempting to read her maladies in these terms. This is especially the case since when Radcliffe was traveling, even to places where the weather would contribute to respiratory problems, she appears to have felt better than when she was confined at home, where she undoubtedly exercised more control over her diet.

Since the journal account provides no details of Radcliffe's health after her return from Ramsgate, here it is necessary to depend on Talfourd, who, in turn, relies on Scudamore, for a description of her final illness. It seems that in the winter, the severe cold caused Radcliffe to relapse. On 9 January 1823, she experienced an attack. Scudamore attended her in vain on 11 January. After becoming temporarily delirious, Radcliffe recovered. Although weak, she was completely sensible. At twelve midnight on February 6, after her husband gave her some refreshment, she uttered her last words ("There is some substance in that") and proceeded to fall asleep. Unable to rouse her, William sent for Scudamore. Before the doctor could reach the house in Stafford Row, Radcliffe had died in her sleep between two and three in the morning on 7 February 1823 at the age of 59. She was interred in a vault at Bayswater in the Chapel of Ease, which belongs to the parish of St. George's, Hanover Square (E131 102-103). Scudamore supplies a detailed account of Radcliffe's death:

> In the early part of January 1823, in consequence of exposure to cold, she was again attacked with inflammation of the lungs, and much more severely than before. Active treatment was immediately adopted, but without the desired relief; and the symptoms soon assumed a most dangerous character. At the end of three weeks, however, and contrary to all expectation, the inflammation of the lungs was overcome; and the amendment was so decided, as to present a slight prospect of recovery.
>
> Alas! our hopes were soon disappointed. Suddenly, in the very moment of seeming calm from the previous violence of disease, a new inflammation seized the membranes of the brain. The enfeebled frame could not resist this fresh assault: so rapid in their course were the violent symptoms, that medical treatment proved wholly unavailing.
>
> In the space of three days, death closed the melancholy scene.
>
> In this manner, at the age of fifty-nine, society was deprived of a most amiable and valuable member, and literature of one of its brightest ornaments.
>
> The foregoing statement will, I hope, afford all the explanation, which can be required, of the nature of Mrs. Radcliffe's illness. During the whole continuance of the inflammation of the lungs, the

mind was perfect in its reasoning powers, and became disturbed only on the last two or three days, as
a natural consequence of the inflammation affecting
the membranes of the brain. (E131 103-104)

So died Ann Radcliffe, the Mother of the female Gothic, remaining
to the end, perhaps appropriately, shrouded in mystery.

Notes

1. Parenthetical references are to entry numbers in the annotated
   bibliography.

2. The signed note, which, at the very least, is useful for deciphering
   Ann's hand in her commonplace book, reads in full:

   > My Dear Miss Williamson,
   >   The carriage is at door, and I have only time
   > to say, that the books are arrived, and that we shall
   > have great pleasure in seeing you on Wednesday.
   > Pray come early, that we may have a ride.
   >   Sincerely Yours,
   >   A Radcliffe

3. Unless otherwise indicated, this biography is based on Talfourd
   (E131).

4. Contemporary spelling and punctuation have been retained to
   preserve the flavor of the originals.

5. The following account of Radcliffe's illness, unless otherwise noted,
   is based on her commonplace book (BPL).

List of Works Cited

Radcliffe, Ann. *The Italian.* Ed. Frederick Garber. 1968. London: Oxford UP, 1989.

Rogers, Deborah D. *Bookseller as Rogue: John Almon and the Politics of Eighteenth-Century Publishing.* NY: Peter Lang, 1986.

_____. "Eighteenth-Century Literary Depictions of Childbirth in the Historical Context of Mutilation and Mortality: The Case of *Pamela*." *Centennial Review* 37 (1993): 305-24.

Woolf, Virginia. "Women and Fiction." *Women and Writing.* Ed. Michèle Barrett. 1929. NY: Harcourt Brace Jovanovich, 1980.

2

PRIMARY BIBLIOGRAPHY: EDITIONS AND TRANSLATIONS (P)

Note: Some of Radcliffe's works printed in America are available in the microprint edition of Early American Imprints published by the American Antiquarian Society.

P1   *THE CASTLES OF ATHLIN AND DUNBAYNE* (1789)

EDITIONS

London: T. Hookham, 1789; Hookham and Carpenter, 1793.

Dublin: Jackson, 1792.

Dublin: H. Colbert, 1794.

Philadelphia: Thomas Bradford, 1796.

Boston: West, 1797.

London: J. Carpenter, 1799.

London: Longman, Hurst, Rees, Orme, and Brown, 1811.

London: J. Jones, 1821.

In Ballantyne's Novelist's Library. Introd. Sir Walter Scott. Edinburgh: James Ballantyne; London: Hurst, Robinson, and Co., 1824. 10: 719-64.

London: Limbird, 1824.

With engravings. West Smithfield: S. Fisher, 1824.

Another edn. London: J. Limbird, 1826.

Another edn. J. Smith, 1836.

Another edn. London: Bruce, 1844.

Another edn. Yorkshire: J.S. Pratt, 1846.

Chiswick: Whittingham, 1827.

London: J.S. Pratt, 1845.

London: J. F. Dove [18—].

Johnson rpt. of 1796 Philadelphia edn., 1970.

Facsim. of 1821 edn. NY: Arno, 1972.

In Devendra Varma's *Complete Novels of Mrs. Ann Radcliffe*. London: The Folio Society, 1987.

TRANSLATIONS

French
Paris: Testu, 1797.
Paris: Plancher, 1819.

P2   *A SICILIAN ROMANCE* (1790)

EDITIONS

London edns. for Hookham/Carpenter published in 1790, 1792, 1796.

Baltimore and Philadelphia: Rice, 1795.

London: Longman, Hurst, Rees, and Orme, 1809.

London: Longman, 1818.

A.K. Newman, Minerva Press, 1820.

London: Fisher and Williams, 1823.

In Ballantyne's Novelist's Library. Introd. Sir Walter Scott. Edinburgh: James Ballantyne; London: Hurst, Robinson, and Co., 1824. 10: 1-74.

West Smithfield: S. Fisher, 1824.

Editions published in London by Limbird in 1824, 1825, and 1826.

London: J.S. Pratt, 1843.

Aberdeen: G. Clark; Dublin: J. M'Glashan, 1848.

> Another edn. [c. 1887].

Johnson rpt. of 1790 Hookham edn., 1971.

Facsim. of 1821 edn. NY: Arno, 1972.

In Devendra Varma's *Complete Novels of Mrs. Ann Radcliffe.* London: The Folio Society, 1987.

NY, Oxford, etc: Oxford UP, 1993.

Facism. of 2nd edn. NY: Woodstock Books, 1995.

TRANSLATIONS

French
Paris: Forget, 1797 and 1798.
Trans. by Moylin Fleury. Paris: Maradan, 1798 and 1819.
Trans. by Fournier. Paris: Michel Lévy frères, 1867.
Other French editions in 1801, 1858, 1860.

German
Trans. by Dorothea Margarethe Liebeskind, Hannover, 1792.

Italian
Milan: Simonetti, 1883.
Milan: Songzogno, 1889.

Russian, 1819.

Spanish
Trans. by I.M.P. Valencia, 1819.

P3   *THE ROMANCE OF THE FOREST* (1791)

EDITIONS

London edns. for T. Hookham and J. Carpenter published in
1791 (2 edns.), 1792, 1794, 1796, 1799.

Dublin edns. for Wogan, Byrne, and others published in 1792,
1793, 1800-1801.

Boston: Samuel Etheridge, 1795.

Philadelphia edns. for Thomas Bradford published in 1795,
1803.

Walpole, NH: Thomas and Thomas, 1806.

London: Longman, Hurst, Rees, and Orme, 1806.

In Mrs. Barbauld's *British Novelists*. London: Rivington,
1810. Vols. 43-44.

A.K. Newman, Minerva Press, 1819.

London: J. Jones, 1820.

In Ballantyne's Novelist's Library. Introd. Sir Walter Scott.
Edinburgh: James Ballantyne; London: Hurst, Robinson, and Co.,
1824. 10: 75-219.

Brattleboro, VT: Holbrook and Fessenden, 1824.

With engravings. West Smithfield: S. Fisher, 1824.

Another edn. London: Limbird, 1824. In Limbird's
British Novelists. Rptd. in 1831.

A new edn. A.K. Newman, 1825.

NY: Duyckinck, 1825.

NY: Published for the booksellers, 1827.

Woodstock, VT: R. Colton, 1832.

Exeter: J & B Williams, 1832 and 1834.

Boston: Clark, 1835.

In penny nos. London: Kelley, 1836.

Another edn., London: 1846.

Another edn., Yorkshire: J.S. Pratt, 1846.

Another edn., London: 1847.

Boston: Bedlington, 1847.

Philadelphia: Leary, 1848.

NY: Derby and Jackson and Cincinnati: H.W. Derby, 1857, 1858, 1860, 1867.

"The Cottage Library," Milner, [1865].

Philadelphia: J.B. Lippincott, 1865.

Another edn., London and NY: 1877.

Under the title *A Father's Crime in Five Fine Old Novels.* Glasgow: Cameron and Ferguson, 1870?

Philadelphia: Claxton, Remsen, and Haffelfinger, 1872.

Adeline; or, The Romance of the Forest. By Mrs. Ann Radcliffe. [Running title: *The Romance of the Forest*] W. Nicholson, 1873?

Another edn., London and NY: 1877.

Philadelphia: J.B. Smith, 187-?

NY and London: Routledge, 1882, [1890?], [1894?], 1904, [n.d.].

In *Half-Forgotten Books.* London: Routledge and NY: E.P. Dutton, 1904; Dutton, 1907.

Abridged in *Three Eighteenth-Century Romances.* NY and Chicago: C. Scribner's Sons, 1931, 1963, 1971.

Facsim. of 1794 edn. NY: Johnson Reprint, 1971.

Repr. of 1791 edn. Ayer, 1974.

Facsim. edn. NY: Arno, 1974.

Oxford, NY, etc.: Oxford UP (World's Classics), 1986.

In Devendra Varma's *Complete Novels of Mrs. Ann Radcliffe.* London: The Folio Society, 1987.

TRANSLATIONS

French
Paris: Denné, 1794; Denné & Poisson, 1796.
Paris: Maradan, 1798.
Trans. by Soulès. Paris: Maradan, 1800, 1802, 1819.
Lecointe et Pougin, 1831.
Trans. by Fournier. Paris: Michel Lévy frères, 1869.

German
Trans. by Dorothea Margarethe Liebeskind. Leipzig, 1793.

Italian
Trans. from Fournier's 1869 version. Milan, 1871.

Russian
Russian translation, possibly of *Romance of the Forest*, Moscow:
1818.

Spanish
Madrid: Razola, 1830.

P4   *THE MYSTERIES OF UDOLPHO* (1794)

EDITIONS

London: G.G. and J. Robinson, 1794 (2 edns.), 1795, 1799,
1803, 1806.

Dublin: Printed for P. Wogan, W. Jones, and H.Colbert, 1794,
1795, 1800.

Boston: Printed by Samuel Etheridge for J. White, W.
Spotswood, Thomas and Andrews, D. West, E. Larkin, W.P.
Blake, J. West, and J.W. Folsom, 1795.

Philadelphia: Rice, 1800.

London: Hurst, Rees and Orme, 1806, 1809.

Paris: T. Barrois, Jr., 1808.

In Mrs. Barbauld's *British Novelists*. London: Rivington,
1810; 1820. Vols. 45-47.

London: 1816.

New Haven: J. Babcock, 1820.

Routledge, [1820?]

Philadelphia: Snall, 1821.

London: S. Fisher, 1823, 1824.

Mason: 1823.

London: J. Limbird, 1824. Afterwards in *Limbird's British Novelist*, 1826, 1832, 1833. Includes Memoir.

In Ballantyne's Novelist's Library. Introd. Sir Walter Scott. Edinburgh: James Ballantyne; London: Hurst, Robinson, and Co., 1824. 10: 221-527. [Radcliffe's five main novels in one vol.]

Philadelphia: J. Woodward, 1828.

London: J.F. Dove, 1830, [185-?]

Exeter, England: J. and B. Williams, 1834, 1837, 1842.

London: Pratt, 1844, 1845.

London: W. Strange, 1844.

Another edn. [c. 1844].

In penny weekly numbers and sixpenny parts. London: Published at *Lloyd's Weekly London Newspaper*, 1846-47.

Philadelphia: Jesper Harding, 1847.

London and Halifax: Milner and Sowerby, [1850?], 1860.

Philadelphia: Gibon, 1851, 1861.

NY: Darby and Jackson, 1857, 1859, 1861.

Philadelphia: J.B. Smith, 1859.

Philadelphia: J.B. Lippincott, 1863.

Philadelphia: Claxton, Remsen, and Haffelfinger, 1869, 1873.

In *The Cottage Library*. London: Milner [1870], 1877.

Philadelphia: E. Claxton, 1881.

London: G. Routledge, 1882.

Half-Forgotten Books. London: Routledge; NY: Dutton [1891?], 1903, 1921, [n.d.].

Everyman's Library. London: J.M. Dent; NY: E.P. Dutton 1931, 1940, 1949, 1959.

Abridged in *Classics of Mystery.* Vol. 7. Juniper Press, 1960.

Abridged (with *Otranto* and *Northanger Abbey*). NY: Holt, 1963.

Oxford, NY, etc.: Oxford UP (World's Classics), 1966, 1970, 1980, 1981, 1983, 1984, 1986, 1988 (rptd. twice), 1989, 1990, 1991.

Philadelphia: Leary and Getz, n.d.

In Devendra Varma's *Complete Novels of Mrs. Ann Radcliffe.* London: The Folio Society, 1987.

TRANSLATIONS

French
Trans. by Victorine de Chastenay. Paris: Maradan, 1797, 1798, 1808, 1819.
Grimvert, 1827.
Pougin, 1839 and 1840.
1849.
Trans. by Fournier. Paris: Michel Lévy frères, 1864 and 1874.
Illustrated by Beaucé, 1869.
Trans. by G. Charbonnier and A. Fréderique. Paris: L'Elan, 1948.
Trans. by Victorine de Chastenay. Revised by A. de Bost. Preface by Marcel Schneider. Paris: P. Belfond, 1966.

German
Trans. by Dorothea Margarethe Liebeskind, 1795, 1798.

Italian
Livorno, 1816-17.
Milan: Fratelli Ferrario, n.d.

Russian, 1905.

P5 *A JOURNEY MADE IN THE SUMMER OF 1794
THROUGH HOLLAND AND THE WESTERN
FRONTIER OF GERMANY WITH A RETURN
DOWN THE RHINE: TO WHICH ARE ADDED
OBSERVATIONS DURING A TOUR TO THE
LAKES OF LANCASHIRE, WESTMORELAND AND
CUMBERLAND* (1795)

EDITIONS

G.G. and J. Robinson, 1795 (2 edns.).

Dublin: Printed by William Porter for Wogan, Byrne, Colbert, Porter, Jones, etc., 1795.

[London: 1814]

Rpt. of 1795 edn. Anglistica and Americana Ser. Hildesheim, Germany: George Olms, 1971.

Ann Arbor: Xerox, University Microfilms [1975].

TRANSLATIONS

French
Trans. by A. Cantwel. Paris, 1795, 1799, 1832.

P6 *THE ITALIAN, OR THE CONFESSIONAL OF THE
BLACK PENITENTS* (1797)

EDITIONS

London: T. Cadell, Jr. and W. Davies, 1797, 1811.

Dublin: P. Wogan, P. Byrne, etc., 1797, 1805.

Philadelphia: Robert Campbell and H. and P. Rice, 1797.

Mount Pleasant, NY: Printed by W. Durell for R. Magill, E. Duyckinck, etc., 1797.

In Ballantyne's Novelist's Library. Introd. Sir Walter Scott. Edinburgh: James Ballantyne; London: Hurst, Robinson, and Co., 1824. 10: 529-717. [Radcliffe's five main novels in one vol.]

London: S. Fisher, 1824.

London: Limbird, 1824, 1826, 1827, 1831.

In *The Illustrated London Novelist.* [c. 1825]

Chiswick: Printed by Whittingham for Arnold, 1826.

London: J. Smith, 1827.

London: Newman, 1828.

In *The Romancist and Novelist's Library.* London: J. Clements, 1840.

London: 1845.

Yorkshire: Pratt, 1846.

Cincinatti: James, 1853.

In *The Cottage Library.* Halifax and London: Milner [c. 1870].

London and NY: 1877.

London: Routledge, 1884.

Published under the title *The Confessional of the Black Peni-tents.* London: Folio Society, 1956.

Facsim. of 1828 edn. NY: Russell and Russell, 1968.

Oxford, NY, etc.: Oxford UP (World's Classics), 1968, 1971, 1981, 1984, 1986, 1987, 1989, 1990, 1991 (twice), 1992.

In Devendra Varma's *Complete Novels of Mrs. Ann Radcliffe.* London: The Folio Society, 1987.

With *Northanger Abbey.* NY: Dutton Signet, 1995.

TRANSLATIONS

French
Paris: Lepetit, 1797, 1799 and 1808.
Trans. by Abbé André Morellet. Paris: Denné, 1797 and Maradan, 1798, 1819.
Other French edns. in 1857, 1858 (two), 1861, and 1863.
Trans. by Fournier. Paris: Michel Lévy frères, 1864.

German
Trans. by Dorothea Margarethe Liebeskind. Konigsberg, 1797
and Leipzig, 1810.
Leipzig and Prague, 1801.

Italian
Milan: Ferrario, n.d.
Trans. by Carlo Sautto. Rome: D. De Luigi, 1944.

Spanish
Barcelona: M. Sauri, 1836.

P7   *THE POEMS OF MRS. ANN RADCLIFFE* (1816)

[Unauthorized selection from her novels]

EDITIONS

London: J. Smith, 1816.

P8   *GASTON DE BLONDEVILLE, OR THE COURT OF
HENRY III KEEPING FESTIVAL IN ARDENNE. A
ROMANCE; ST. ALBANS ABBEY. A METRICAL
TALE* [Prefixed by a memoir of Radcliffe and
extracts from her journals] (Posthumously, 1826)

EDITIONS

London: Henry Colburn, 1826, 1833, 1834, 1839.

Vols. 3 and 4 reissued as *The Poetical Works.* London: Printed by
H. Colburn for R. Bentley, 1834. Rptd. by AMS Press, 1992-93.

Philadelphia: Carey and Lea, 1826.

NY: Collins and Rannay, Duyckinck, etc., 1826.

Facsim. of 1826 edn. *Gaston de Blondeville* (only) with Memoir. NY: Arno, 1972.

Facsim. of 1826 edn. Ann Arbor: University Microfilms, 1972.

Rpt. of 1826 edn. Anglistica and Americana Ser. Hildesheim,
Germany: George Olms, 1976.

In Devendra Varma's *Complete Novels of Mrs. Ann Radcliffe.* London: The Folio Society, 1987.

TRANSLATIONS

French
Trans. A.J.B. Defauconpret. Paris: Mâme & Delaunay Vallée, 1826.

P9   "ON THE SUPERNATURAL IN POETRY" (in *New Monthly Magazine,* posthumously, 1826)

COLLECTIONS

[Works] London: G.G. and J. Robinson, 1797-1811. 13 vols. in 14.

Radcliffe, Ann. *Ann Radcliffe: The Novels.* Hildesheim, Germany: Georg Olms, 1974.

Other collections are integrated and appear under individual titles.

3

EARLY REVIEWS AND NOTICES,
1789–1826 (E)

Note: In years with reviews, other notices precede reviews. Parodies and adaptations appear in a separate section.

1789

REVIEWS AND NOTICES OF *THE CASTLES OF ATHLIN AND DUNBAYNE*

E1 Rev. of *The Castles of Athlin and Dunbayne. Critical Review* 68 (1789): 251.

Mixed review criticizes the author (assumed to be male) for inauthentic rendering of the Highlands.

E2 M. Rev. of *The Castles of Athlin and Dunbayne. Scots Magazine* 51 (1789): 645.

Brief review says this work is "To be commended for its moral; as also for the good sentiments and reflections which occasionally occur in it."

E3 Rev. of *The Castles of Athlin and Dunbayne. Monthly Review* 81 (1789): 563.

Negative review implicitly finds that this novel will appeal to women and to children, that is, to "the young and unformed mind. To men who have passed, or even attained, the meridian of life, a series of events, which seem not to have their foundation in nature, will ever be insipid, if not disgustful."

Nevertheless, admires the moral.

E4   Rev. of *The Castles of Athlin and Dunbayne. Town and Country Magazine* 21 (1789): 469.

Brief notice finds the work imaginative, although "the author is totally unacquainted with the manners of the people among whom he lays his scene."

1790

REVIEWS AND NOTICES OF *A SICILIAN ROMANCE*

[See also *Critical Review*, 1791]

E5   Carter, Elizabeth. Letter to Mrs. Montagu dated 15 December 1790. *Letters from Mrs. Elizabeth Carter to Mrs. Montagu, between the Years 1755 and 1800.* Ed. Montagu Pennington. 3 vols. London: Printed for F.C. and J. Rivington, 1817. 3: 322-25.

Praises *Sicilian Romance.* Does not know who the author (assumed to be female) is.

E6   D°. Rev. of *A Sicilian Romance. Monthly Review* ns 3 (1790): 91.

Positive review praises originality and decorum.

E7   Rev. of *A Sicilian Romance. General Magazine* 4 (1790): 318.

Brief positive review finds the novel full of "rich effusions" that "cannot fail to affect the hearts of those who are possessed of feeling and taste."

E8   M. Rev. of *A Sicilian Romance. Scots Magazine* 52 (1790): 438.

Brief review finds the style used to describe romantic and suprising incidents lively and elegant.

1791

E9   Rev. of *A Sicilian Romance. Critical Review* 2nd ser. 1 (1791): 350.

Finds the novel entertaining despite improbabilities.

1792

REVIEWS AND NOTICES OF *ROMANCE OF THE FOREST*

E10   Rev. of *The Romance of the Forest. Critical Review* 2nd ser. 4 (1792): 458-60.

Favorable review compares this novel with *The Old English Baron.*

E11   Rev. of *The Romance of the Forest. English Review* 20 (1792): 352-53.

Favorable review with extract praises "the fair author" (352) for her originality, descriptions, characterization, and incidents, which *"o'erstep not the modesty of nature"* (352).

E12   Rev. of *The Romance of the Forest. Monthly Review* ns 8 (1792): 82-87.

Praise for the way Radcliffe engages the attention and builds suspense.

E13   Rev. of *The Romance of the Forest. Scots Magazine* 54 (1792): 292.

Brief favorable review praises the novel for capturing attention and arousing emotions. Adapted from *Monthly Review.*

1794

[See also Smith, 1796.]

E14   Walpole, Horace. Letter to Lady Ossory dated 4 September 1794. *Horace Walpole's Correspondence with the Countess of Upper Ossory.* Ed. W.S. Lewis and A. Dayle Wallace with the assistance of Edwine M. Martz. New Haven: Yale UP, 1965. 3:202-204.

Reference to "mothers" undoubtedly includes Radcliffe:

> I have read some of the descriptive verbose tales, of which your Ladyship says I was the patriarch by several mothers. All I can say for myself, is, that I do not think my concubines have produced issue more natural for excluding the aid of anything marvellous. (3:204)

REVIEWS AND NOTICES OF *UDOLPHO*

E15   A.Y. [Dyer, George?] Rev. of *The Mysteries of Udolpho. Analyti-*
       cal Review 19 (1794): 140-45.

       Positive review with long plot summary and extracts. For
       attribution see Roper (1972).

E16   Rev. of *The Mysteries of Udolpho. British Critic* 4 (1794): 110-21.

       High praise for *Udolpho* as one of Radcliffe's best novels.
       Objects to interspersed verses, which detract from the narra-
       tive. Includes detailed plot summary with extracts.

E17   [Coleridge, Samuel Taylor?] Rev. of *Udolpho. Critical Review*
       2nd ser. 11 (1794): 361-72.

       Criticizes Radcliffe's anachronisms, redundancy, and use of
       suspense, cautioning that "in the search of what is new, an
       author is apt to forget what is natural; and, in rejecting the
       more obvious conclusions, to take those which are less satis-
       factory" (362). Finds that "the reader, when he is got to the
       end of the work, looks about in vain for the spell which had
       bound him so strongly to it" (362).

       Although this review was once widely attributed to Coleridge,
       his authorship has recently been questioned. For the debate
       about attribution, see Patterson (1951), Erdman (1959), and
       Roper (1972).

E18   [Enfield, William.] Rev. of *The Mysteries of Udolpho. The Monthly*
       Review ns 15 (1794): 278-83.

       Favorable review praises Radcliffe's good judgment, picturesque
       descriptions (even though they occur too frequently), charac-
       terization, explanations of mysteries, inventiveness and "en-
       chanting power" (279) to excite terror. Wishes the verses had
       appeared separately. Attributed to Enfield by Ioan Williams.

E19   Rev. of *The Mysteries of Udolpho. English Review* 23 (1794): 464-68.

       Review consists of plot summary and quotations. Concludes
       with praise: "In this romance are interspersed some beautiful
       pieces of poetry. . . . The interest of the story is wonderfully
       well kept up; the imagery is picturesque, and sometimes sub-
       lime; but, on the whole, is rather crowded.—This is the best
       composition of this kind that has appeared since Mrs.
       Inchbald's Simple Story" (468).

E20   Rev. of *The Mysteries of Udolpho. European Magazine and London Review* 25 (1794): 433-40.

Extended plot summary with excerpts. Predicts that "This Romance . . . as long as such productions shall continue to have any power over the imagination, will stand high, we doubt not, in the public favour" (440). Objects to minute descriptions.

E21   Farington, Joseph. Entry for 15 September 1794. *The Farington Diary.* Ed. James Greig. 8 vols. London: Hutchinson, 1923-28. 1:71.

Briefly comments on Elizabeth Carter's favorable opinion of *Udolpho:* "Lady B. [Beaumont] recd. a letter to-day from Mrs Carter, who expresses herself in a very strong manner in favor of the *'Mysteries of Udolpho'* and of the talents of Mrs. Radcliffe, the author."

Quotes Haynes Bayley:

> O Radcliffe! Thou once wert the charmer
> Of girls, who sat reading all night:
> Thy heroes were striplings in armour,
> Thy heroines damsels in white.
> But past are thy terrible touches.

E22   Rev. of *The Mysteries of Udolpho. Gentleman's Magazine* 64, Pt. 2 (1794): 834.

Overall positive review but objects to frequency of landscape descriptions. If the plot is too drawn out, it is too hastily concluded.

E23   Lewis, Matthew G. Letter to his mother dated 18 May 1794. *The Life and Correspondence of M.G. Lewis.* 2 vols. London: Henry Colburn, 1839. 1: 122-24.

Recommends *Udolpho,* which inspired him to continue *The Monk.* Wonders if he resembles Montoni. Editorial comment that follows this letter observes that ". . . the pen of Ann Radcliffe showed no little share of masculine strength" (1:125).

E24   Mathias, Thomas James. *The Pursuits of Literature. A Satirical Poem in Four Dialogues.* 1794. 6th ed. London: Printed for T. Becket, 1798.

Compares "the mighty magician of THE MYSTERIES OF
UDOLPHO" to Smith, Inchbald, and Robinson, who are "too
frequently *whining* or *frisking* in novels, till our girls' heads
turn wild with impossible adventures, and now and then are
tainted with democracy" (20n).

E25   *Udolpho* listed in *New Annual Register* 15 (1794): 257.

E26   Piozzi, Hester Lynch. Entry for 20 August 1794. *Thraliana:
The Diary of Mrs. Hester Lynch Thrale (Later Mrs. Piozzi).* Ed.
Katharine C. Balderston. Oxford: Clarendon Press, 1942.
2:885-87.

Refers to reading *Udolpho*: "We have all been reading the
Mysteries of Udolpho; 'tis very horrible indeed says one, very
like Macbeth says another: Yes truly replied H:L:P. as like as
Pepper-Mint Water is to good Brandy" (2:886).

E27   Piozzi, Hester Lynch. Note of 2 December 1794. Qtd. in
Clifford, James. *Hester Lynch Piozzi (Mrs. Thrale).* 1941. NY:
Columbia UP, 1987.

"The reading Ladies of Denbigh find our Mysteries of
Udolpho a Treasure, I sent for it from London to divert
them. Cecilia says that like Emily the moment my Mind or
my Teeth are at Ease for an Instant, I set about *arranging* a
few Stanzas . . ." (379).

E28   *Udolpho* listed under "New Publications" in *Scots Magazine* 56
(1794): 771.

E29   Seward, Anna. Letter to C. Smyth dated 3 August 1794. *Letters of Anna Seward: Written between the Years 1784 and 1807.* 6
vols. Edinburgh: Printed by George Ramsay for Archibald
Constable and Company, Edinburgh; and Longman, Hurst,
Rees, etc., London, 1811. 3:388-90.

Although objects to "the Novel trash of the day" (3: 389),
finds Radcliffe worthwhile. Prefers *Udolpho* to *Romance of the
Forest.* Admires Radcliffe's scenic descriptions but finds them
overabundant.

1795

E30   D'Arblay, Fanny (Fanny Burney). Letter to Dr. Burney dated
18 June 1795. *Diary and Letters of Madame d'Arblay.* Ed. Charlotte Barrett. Preface and notes by Austin Dobson. 6 vols.

1842. Revised edn. NY and London: Macmillan, 1905. 5: 263-66.

Alludes to Radcliffe in the course of discussing what was to be called *Camilla*: "I like well the idea of giving no name at all,—why should not I have my mystery as well as Udolpho?" (5: 264)

REVIEWS AND NOTICES OF *A JOURNEY*

[See also Green, 1800.]

E31   Rev. of *A Journey Made in the Summer of 1794. Critical Review* 2nd ser. 14 (1795): 241-55.

Effusive praise of the *Journey* for its reflections and descriptions. Registers some regret for lack of illustrations. Includes long extract.

E32   E.D. Rev. of *A Journey Made in the Summer of 1794. Analytical Review* 22 (1795): 349-55.

Fairly favorable review finds this work less interesting than Radcliffe's romances.

E33   Rev. of *A Journey Made in the Summer of 1794. English Review* 26 (July, Aug. and Sept. 1795): 1-5, 89-90, 173-78.

Praises descriptions of natural scenery, which seem to be produced by a landscape painter, but objects that nature cannot be translated into words and that Radcliffe describes areas many travellers have already detailed. Also finds fault with lack of illustrations.

E34   Rev. of *A Journey Made in the Summer of 1794. European Magazine and London Review* 28 (Aug. and Oct. 1795): 98-103, 257-61.

Praises Radcliffe's descriptions, which are good enough "to accomplish that by the pen which has always been considered as belonging necessarily to the province of the pencil" (99).

E35   Rev. of *A Journey Made in the Summer of 1794. Monthly Review* ns 18 (1795): 241-46.

Praises Radcliffe for her truthful descriptions. Includes long excerpt.

E36   *A Journey Made in the Summer of 1794* listed in *Scots Magazine*
           57 (1795): 382.

                                        1796

E37   Rev. of *The Italian. English Review* 28 (Dec. 1796): 574-79.

           Negative review of the novel as "a complication of horrors
           without interest" (574), which suffers from succeeding
           Udolpho. Criticizes repetitious pastoral scenes.

E38   *The Italian* listed in *Monthly Magazine* 2 (Dec. 1796): 899.

E39   Lansdell, Sarah. *Manfredi, Baron St. Osmund.* 2 vols. London:
           Printed for W. Lane at the Minerva Press, 1796.

           Introduction pays homage to Radcliffe: "It may be considered
           as presumption in a young authoress to venture her little pro-
           ductions abroad in the world, when there are so many works
           extant of Radcliffe's, Smith's, Bennett's, and Burney's, who so
           greatly excel in this species of composition" (1:vi).

E40   Rev. of *Mysteries Elucidated. Critical Review* 16 (1796): 359.

           Defends Radcliffe from implied criticism.

E41   Seward, Anna. Letter 29 to Eleanor Butler dated 4 February
           1796. *Letters of Anna Seward Written between the Years 1784 and
           1807.* 6 vols. Edinburgh: Printed by George Ramsay for
           Archibald Constable and Company, Edinburgh; and
           Longman, Hurst, Rees, etc., London, 1811. 4: 149-152.

           Praises Radcliffe's *Tour* and suggests a relationship between
           the *Tour* and *Udolpho* (4:150-51).

E42   Smith, Elihu Hubbard. Letters to Mary S. Mumford, his sis-
           ter, dated 1796. *The Diary of Elihu Hubbard Smith.* Ed. James
           E. Cronin. Philadelphia: American Philosophical Society,
           1973. 181-82 and 225-26.

           Letter dated 28 June 1796 (181-82) criticizes the explained
           supernatural in *Udolpho*: "It appears the labour of a Moun-
           tain, to bring forth a mouse" (182). (Anna Seward played on
           this analogy in 1799.)

           Letter dated 4 October 1796 (225-26): Apparently in response
           to her defense of *Udolpho*, Smith urges his sister, "Beware of
           false impressions!" (226)

1797

E43   Farington, Joseph. Entry for 28 August 1797. *The Farington Diary*. Ed. James Greig. 8 vols. London: Hutchinson, 1923-28. 1:214.

Mistaking the age of Ann, who must have been thirty-three at the time, relays some personal observations about the Radcliffes:

> Marchi called—He dined yesterday with Mr & Mrs Radcliffe the Authoress—She is daughter to Mr Ward who was a Bookseller at Bath. Mrs Radcliffe is 27 or 8 years old, a pretty face. Marchi told her of Johnson & Goldsmith coming to Sir Joshua Reynolds, she said, those were fine times. Mr Radcliffe was educated at Oxford—He is now Editor of an Evening paper, for which He paid £1000—He is abt. 30 years old and democratically inclined. They reside at No. 7 Medina Place—St. Georges fields.

E44   Fox, [Joseph]. *Santa-Maria; or, The Mysterious Pregnancy*. 3 vols. London: G. Kearsley, 1797.

Prefatory Epistle mentions Radcliffe.

E45   Rev. of Fox's *Santa Maria, or the Mysterious Pregnancy*. *Monthly Mirror* 4 (1797): 38-39.

Describes Fox as a "pupil of the Radcliffe school" (38), whose novel has all of Radcliffe's defects but none of her beauties.

E46   Green, Thomas. Entry for 1 February 1797. *Extracts from The Diary of a Lover of Literature*. Ipswich: Printed and sold by John Raw, 1810.

Prefers Radcliffe to Walpole because she "evokes scenes of far more thrilling horror . . . "(23).

E47   Rev. of *Joscelina* by Isabella Kelly. *Monthly Mirror* 4 (1797): 218.

Finds the novel highly derivative: "The materials are borrowed, with an ill grace, from Radcliffe and Sterne."

E48   Rev. of *The Monk*. *Monthly Review* 23 (1797): 451.

Finds *The Monk* unoriginal. Descriptions of the convent prison were derived from Radcliffe.

E49   Note appended to a letter on "Terrorist Novel Writing" in *The Spirit of Public Journals* (1797) 1:323.

Unseen. Quoted by MacCarthy to suggest Radcliffe compensating for lack of education.

E50   Tyler, Royall. *The Algerine Captive.* 1797. Introd. Jack A. Moore. 2 vols. in one. Gainesville: Scholars' Facsimiles and Reprints, 1967.

Preface ironically comments on the taste for entertaining literature among farmers: ". . . Dolly the dairy maid, and Jonathan the hired man . . . amused themselves into so agreeable a terror with the haunted houses and hobgoblins of Mrs. Ratcliffe [*sic*], that they were both afraid to sleep alone" (ix).

REVIEWS AND NOTICES OF *THE ITALIAN*

[See also *English Review* (1796), *Monthly Magazine* (1796), Coleridge's review (1798), and *Anti-Jacobin Review* (1800).]

E51   [Aikin, Arthur.] Rev. of *The Italian. Monthly Review* ns 22 (1797): 282-84.

Although the realistic novel is superior to the Romance, *The Italian* occupies "a very distinguished rank among the modern works of fiction" (283). Attributed to Aikin by Ioan Williams. Includes long excerpt.

E52   Rev. of *The Italian* (with long excerpt) in *British Critic* 10 (1797): 266-70.

Favorable review praises landscapes and characterization, especially of Schedoni.

E53   Coleridge, Samuel Taylor. Letter to William Lisle Bowles. March (?) 1797. *A Wiltshire Parson and his Friends: The Correspondence of William Lisle Bowles: Together with Four Hitheto Unidentified Reviews by Coleridge.* Ed. Garland Greever. London: Constable, 1926. 29-31.

Coleridge acknowledges his review of *The Italian* (which itself contains a reference to his previous review of *Udolpho*) for *Critical Review.*

> . . . I am almost weary of the terrible, having been an hireling in the Critical Review for these last six or

eight months—I have been lately reviewing the Monk, the Italian, Hubert de Sevrac, &c &c &c—in all of which dungeons, and old castles, and solitary Houses by the Sea Side, and Caverns, and Woods, and extraordinary characters, and all the tribe of Horror and Mystery, have crowded on me—even to surfeiting. (30)

E54 Rev. of *The Italian. European Magazine* 31 (1797): 35.

Negative review objects to the "wild extravagancies" and finds the character of the monk revolting.

E55 Green, Thomas. Entry for 25 March 1797. *Extracts from The Diary of a Lover of Literature*. Ipswich: Printed and sold by John Raw, 1810. 28.

Finds *The Italian* similar to Radcliffe's other works. Praises her picturesque and terrifying descriptions but criticizes her improbabilities, characterization, and "development of those mysteries which have kept us stretched so long on the rack of terror and impatience. . . ."

E56 Rev. of *The Italian. Monthly Magazine* 4 (1797): 120-21.

Praises *The Italian* for "picturesque descriptions, singular characters, wonderful incidents, and delineations of over-powering passion."

E57 Rev. of *The Italian. Monthly Mirror* 3 (1797): 155-58.

Favorable review (with extended plot summary) of *The Italian* as an improvement on Radcliffe's previous romances. Applauds the fact that "The reader of the *Italian* is not perpetually harrassed with overcharged descriptions of the beauties of nature . . ." (155). Praises characterization, especially that of Schedoni. Ellena combines "female delicacy and innocence, with a manly dignity and firmness" (157).

E58 Rev. of *The Italian. Monthly Visitor* 1 (1797): 79-85.

Consisting mostly of plot summary and extracts, this review concludes that Radcliffe's delineation of Schedoni and her creation of fear are impressive, even if her descriptions are verbose.

E59 *The Italian* listed in *Scots Magazine* 59 (1797): 266.

E60   [Wollstonecraft, Mary?] Rev. of *The Italian. Analytical Review*
            25 (1797): 516-20.

            Praises *The Italian* more for its parts than for the whole.
            Radcliffe's "improving judgment" (516) is evident in the pic-
            turesque descriptions, which are more concise, and the re-
            flections, which are more frequent. Objects to improbabili-
            ties: "We are made to wonder, only to wonder; but the spell,
            by which we are led, again and again, round the same magic
            circle, is the spell of genius" (516). Includes long excerpt.

                                    1798

E61   [Coleridge, Samuel Taylor?] Rev. of *The Italian. Critical Re-
            view* 2nd ser. 23 (1798): 166-69.

            Negative review includes long extract. In general finds the
            Romance inferior to the realistic novel. *Udolpho* is inferior to
            Romance of the Forest because of its protracted incidents and
            redundant description. *The Italian* is inferior to *Udolpho* be-
            cause of its scenes and characters, which are the same as in
            Udolpho. Although the descriptions are more concise, they
            are at times irrelevant.

            Widely attributed to Coleridge. See Coleridge's 1797 letter
            to Bowles above. Attribution rejected by Patterson (1951),
            accepted by Erdman (1959).

E62   Drake, Nathan. "On Objects of Terror." *Literary Hours: or
            Sketches, Critical, Narrative, and Poetical.* 1798. 4th ed. 3 vols.
            London: Printed for Longman, Hurst, Rees, Orme, and
            Brown, 1820. 1:269-84.

            Characterizes Radcliffe as "the Shakspeare [*sic*] of Romance
            Writers" (1: 273). Praises *The Italian.* Admires Radcliffe's ter-
            rific scenes, which are softened so that they never turn into
            horror, "but pleasurable emotion is ever the predominating
            result" (1: 274).

E63   *Heir of Montague.* London: Minerva Press, 1798.

            The hero praises *Romance of the Forest*, faulting it for being
            too short. His friend replies, "It made me melancholy a week;
            I did not think it had been in the power of a book to affect
            me so much."

E64 Rev. of *The Libertines. British Critic* 12 (1798): 670.

Radcliffe is the standard of comparison for this novel, which is "more gloomy and terrible than even the Italian of Mrs. Radcliffe."

E65 Rivers, David. "Radcliffe, Mrs. Ann." *Literary Memoirs of Living Authors of Great Britain.* 2 vols. London: Printed for R. Faulder, 1798. 2: 181-82.

Finds *Udolpho* and *Romance of the Forest* Radcliffe's most popular and admired novels. Praises Radcliffe, who ranks "among the first novel-writers of her age . . ." (2: 181). Admires her verses interspersed in the novels. The *Journey* "adds a new laurel to the brows of the fair writer" (2: 182).

E66 Robinson, Henry Crabb. Letter to William Pattisson dated 22 April 1798. *Henry Crabb Robinson on Books and their Writers.* Ed. Edith J. Morley. 3 vols. 1938. AMS Press, 1967. [Partially published earlier as *Diary, Reminiscences, and Correspondence* (1869).] 3:843.

Robinson has re-read *Udolpho* "with Delight" (3: 843). Years later, in 1829, he is less enthusiastic.

1799

E67 [Cooke, Cassandra.] *Battleridge: an Historical Tale, Founded on Facts.* 2 vols. London: Cawthorn, 1799.

Preface praises Radcliffe, dubbing her "Queen of the *tremendous*" (1:viii). Objects to imitators.

E68 Rev. of Elizabeth (Gunning) Plunkett's *The Gipsey Countess. British Critic* 14 (1799): 549.

Praises Gunning, while ranking her below Radcliffe and Burney.

E69 *Reginald, or The House of Mirandola.* 3 vols. London: Printed at the Minerva Press for William Lane, 1799.

Preface pays homage to Radcliffe.

E70 Seward, Anna. Letter 41 to Rev. T.S. Whalley dated 7 June 1799. *Letters of Anna Seward Written between the Years 1784 and 1807.* 6 vols. Edinburgh: Printed by George Ramsay for Archibald Constable and Company, Edinburgh; and Longman, Hurst, Rees, etc., London, 1811. 5: 239-45.

Criticizes Radcliffe's lack of realism and emphasis on sensational effects: "One has heard of a labouring mountain bringing forth a mouse: In Mrs R.'s writings mice bring forth mountains" (5: 244). (See Elihu Smith, 1796.)

1800

E71 Bisset, Robert. *Douglas; or, The Highlander. A Novel.* 4 vols. Dublin: Printed by W. Porter for P. Wogan, 1800.

Preface praises Radcliffe, while criticizing her imitators.

E72 Coleridge, Samuel Taylor. "The Mad Monk." 1800. *The Poems of Samuel Taylor Coleridge.* Ed. Ernest Hartley Coleridge. NY: Oxford UP, 1924. 347-49.

Originally published in the *Morning Post* under the title "The Voice from the Side of Etna; or the Mad Monk: An Ode in Mrs. Ratcliff's [*sic*] Manner."

E73 [Dubois, Robert]. *St Godwin: A Tale of the Sixteenth, Seventeenth, and Eighteenth Century.* By Count Reginald de St. Leon. London: J. Wright, 1800.

Parody of *St Leon* mocks Godwin's descriptions by invoking Radcliffe: "I wish I had Mrs. Radcliffe by me, for I am at a stand; I know this is the place for description, but I cannot get on" (29).

E74 Green, Thomas. Entry for 26 May 1800. *Extracts from The Diary of a Lover of Literature.* Ipswich: Printed and sold by John Raw, 1810. 225.

Green is surprisingly pleased by Radcliffe's Tour to the Lakes.

E75 Green, Thomas. Entry for 25 November 1800 from manuscript intended as a continuation of *Extracts*, but Green died before publication. In *Gentleman's Magazine* 104 (1834): 5-16:

Radcliffe improved upon the descriptions from Hester Lynch Piozzi's (Mrs. Thrale's) *Observations and Reflections*: "Read the first volume of Mrs. *Piozzi's* Travels in Italy. . . . Mrs. *Radcliffe* has taken from this work her vivid description of Venice, and of the Brenta, but oh! how improved in the transcript" (10).

E76 Rev. of *The Italian. Anti-Jacobin Review* 7 (1800): 27-30.

Reviewer has "weighty objections" since considers Schedoni

as the real hero of the novel. Finds *The Italian* inferior to Radcliffe's other works.

E77   Untitled. *Literary Leisure* No. 56 (1800): 304-11.

Praises Radcliffe but criticizes her imitators.

E78   Sade, Donatien Alphonse François, comte de (known as the Marquis de Sade). "Reflections on the Novel." Introductory essay for *Les Crimes de l'Amour* (1800). *The 120 Days of Sodom and Other Writings.* Trans. Austryn Wainhouse and Richard Seaver. NY: Grove Weidenfeld, 1966: 91-116.

Briefly discusses English Gothics: "[F]oremost among them I would place *The Monk*, which is superior in all respects to the strange flights of Mrs. Radcliffe's brilliant imagination. . . . [T]his kind of fiction, whatever one may think of it, is assuredly not without merit: 'twas the inevitable result of the revolutionary shocks which all of Europe has suffered. . . . [T]o compose works of interest, one had to call upon the aid of hell itself . . . "(108-109).

1801

E79   Rev. of *The Mysterious Penitent* (1800). *British Critic* 17 (1801): 541.

Radcliffe held up as the standard of comparison.

1802

E80   Kett, Henry. *Elements of General Knowledge.* 1802 (?) Philadelphia: Printed by H. Maxwell for F. Nichols and J.A. Cummings, 1805.

Includes Radcliffe in list of luminaries such as Bacon, Newton, Addison, and Locke.

1803

E81   "To Readers and Correspondents." *Port Folio* 3 (1803): 375.

Reports rumors of a new Radcliffe novel in the works: "It has been rumoured that Mrs. Radcliffe has for some time been engaged in the composition of a Romance, of a very superior cast."

E82   Porter, Jane. *Thaddeus of Warsaw.* London: Printed by A.
            Strahan for T.N. Longman and O. Rees, 1803.

            Mentions Radcliffe's "elegant pages."

                                      1804

E83   [Brown, Charles Brockden?] "On a Taste for the Picturesque."
            Literary Magazine and American Register 2 (1804): 163-65.

            Speaker in dialogue praises Radcliffe as "the most illustrious
            of the picturesque writers" (165). Faults critics who focus
            only on her characterization.

E84   Irving, Washington. Entries for 1804. *Journals and Notebooks.*
            Ed. Nathalia Wright. Madison: U of Wisconsin P, 1969.

            Entry for 8 August 1804 (1:55-60) finds Irving reminded of
            Radcliffe when he sees an old castle while traveling in France:
            "The discriptions [*sic*] of Mrs. Radcliffe were brought imme-
            diately to my reccollection [*sic*]. this would have formed a
            fine picture for her talents to work upon" (1: 55-56).

            Entry for 9 October 1804 (·1:488-89): "The french physician
            was so much interested in Mrs Radcliffes Romance of the
            Italian—translated in french which I had lent him that he
            read it all the road & had nearly broken his head against
            several walls & trees which he encountered" (1:489).

E85   Piozzi, Hester Lynch (Mrs. Thrale). Entry for 11 October
            1804. *Thraliana: The Diary of Mrs. Hester Lynch Thrale (Later
            Mrs. Piozzi).* Ed. Katharine C. Balderston. Oxford: Clarendon
            Press, 1942. 2:1060-62.

            Refers to book review of *Azemia* in *The Monthly Mirror* that
            accuses the novel of satirizing Piozzi and Radcliffe, among
            others.

                                      1805

E86   Murray, Hugh. *Morality of Fiction.* Edinburgh: Printed by
            Mundell and Son for Longman, Hurst, Rees, and Orme, Lon-
            don; and A. Constable and Co. and J. Anderson, Edinburgh,
            1805. 126-28.

            Radcliffe's representations of villains are striking, as are her
            scenes of terror. Although Murray cannot deny the pleasure

the latter afford, he objects on moral grounds that it is "not of a very high order; and, till her time, was confined chiefly to the nursery. Nor is it of a very improving nature, but, on the contrary, tends rather to weaken the mind, and make it liable to superstitious apprehensions" (127).

1806

E87 "On Novels and Romances, with a Cursory Review of the Literary Ladies of Great-Britain." *Belle Assemblée* 1 (1806): 531-33.

Includes notice of Radcliffe.

1807

E88 Rev. of Duff's *Letters on the Intellectual and Moral Character of Women*. *British Critic* 30 (1807): 544-47.

Reviewer uses example of Radcliffe to argue against Duff's belief that women are too delicate to create supernatural characters: "On what principle of the science of human nature he, who has read or even heard of the works of Mrs. Radcliffe, can contend that the *delicate organization* of the female form is 'obstructive of the talent of inventing and exhibiting supernatural characters, with their proper insignia and attributes,' we cannot conceive . . ." (544).

E89 Lathom, Francis. *Human Beings*. London: Printed for B. Crosby by J. and E. Hodson, 1807.

Preface refers briefly to Radcliffe.

1808

E90 Lamb, Charles. Letter 223 to William Godwin dated March, 1808. *The Letters of Charles and Mary Anne Lamb*. Ed. Edwin W. Marrs, Jr. Ithaca and London: Cornell UP, 1976. 2:279.

Lamb indicates the continuing popularity of *Udolpho*, insisting that "such things **sell**."

1809

E91 Obituary. *Gentleman's Magazine* 79, Pt. 1 (1809): 188.

Obituary of seventy-one-year-old Deborah Radcliffe, Ann Radcliffe's mother-in-law.

1810

E92   Barbauld, Mrs. Anna Letitia (Aiken). "Mrs. Radcliffe." Introductory Preface. *The British Novelists.* 50 vols. London: Printed
for Rivington and others, 1810. 43: i-viii.

Places Radcliffe at the top of the class of romance writers.
Romance of the Forest is one of her best works. La Motte's
character is "drawn with spirit" (43: ii). *Udolpho,* Radcliffe's
most popular work, is similar to *Romance of the Forest* in its
incidents and in the emotions it excites, but characters are
less fully developed. *Udolpho* has a more complicated, imper-
fect story, whose ending does not depend enough on previous circumstances. Although the apparent supernatural is
explained, it is not always explained satisfactorily, leaving
the reader disappointed. Prefers *The Italian* (which she mistakenly calls *The Sicilian*) to *Udolpho.* Praises characterization
of Schedoni. Although readers get caught up in the suspense
while reading Radcliffe, they have no desire to reread her
novels: "[W]e are ashamed of our feelings, and do not wish
to recall them" (vii). Praises Radcliffe's descriptions as well
as her poetry, which, Barbauld fears, gets lost in the novels.

E93   Coleridge, Samuel Taylor. Letter 808 to William Wordsworth.
Early Oct. 1810. *Collected Letters of Samuel Taylor Coleridge.* Ed.
Earl Leslie Griggs. 4 vols. Oxford: Clarendon Press, 1956. 3:
290-96.

Coleridge provides a formula for romances in Radcliffe's style.

1813

E94   Robinson, Henry Crabb. Journal entries for 5 April 1813
(1:122), 20 March 1813 (1:124), and 2 August 1813 (1: 130).
Henry Crabb Robinson on Books and their Writers. Ed. Edith J.
Morley. 3 vols. 1938. AMS Press, 1967. [Partially published
earlier as *Diary, Reminiscences, and Correspondence* (1869).]

Entries briefly mention Radcliffe.

1814

E95   Austen, Jane. Letter to Cassandra Austen. 2 March 1814.
Jane Austen's Letters to her Sister Cassandra and Others. Ed. R.W.
Chapman. 2 vols. Oxford: Clarendon Press, 1932. 2:375-78.

Refers to Barrett's *The Heroine* as "a delightful burlesque, particularly on the Radcliffe style" (2: 377).

E96   Dunlop, John Colin. *History of Prose Fiction*. Ed. Henry Wilson. 2 vols. 1814. [First published in 1814 under the title *History of Fiction*.] London: George Bell and Sons, 1888. 2:580-86.

Widely quoted by early critics, Dunlop, in what he claimed was the first history of English fiction, praises Radcliffe's terrific scenes but criticizes her digressive dialogue and inadequate explanations of mysteries. In *Udolpho* the reader is "disappointed and disgusted to find that all this pother has been raised by an image of wax!" (2: 581) Her picturesque descriptions are beautiful, but too frequent. *Romance of the Forest* is more interesting than *Udolpho* or *The Italian* although some scenes in *The Italian* are unsurpassed by Shakespeare. Radcliffe's heroines are too similar: "They have all blue eyes and auburn hair. . . . Unfortunately they are all likewise early risers" (2: 581).

E97   Rev. of John Dunlop's *History of Fiction*. *British Critic* ns 2 (1814): 164-80.

In Johnsonian tones reviewer finds the stature of Richardson, Fielding, Smollett, Burney, and Radcliffe fixed, to be neither "exalted nor depressed by the praise or censure of the present day" (179). Observes problems with rereading Radcliffe: "Means and agents, apparently supernatural, cease to interest, when they cease to astonish; and all the terror and suspense created by the mysterious chamber is tedious and trifling at the second reading, when every marvel, in succession, will be dissipated by the recollection of the waxen figure. . . . Radcliffe is read once with breathless interest, but only twice without fatigue" (180).

E98   Scott, Sir Walter. *Waverley: or 'Tis Sixty Years Since*. 1814. NY: Peter Fenelon Collier and Son, 1892.

Chapter one mocks Radcliffe's style in a defense of Scott's subtitle: "Had I . . . announced in my frontispiece, 'Waverley, a Tale of other Days,' must not every novel-reader have anticipated a castle scarce less than that of Udolpho, of which the eastern wing had long been uninhabited, and the keys either lost, or consigned to the care of some aged butler or housekeeper, whose trembling steps, about the middle of the second volume, were doomed to guide the hero, or heroine, to the ruinous precincts? Would not the owl have shrieked, and the cricket cried in my very title-page? and could it have been possible for me, with moderate attention to decorum, to introduce any scene more lively than might be produced by the jocularity of a clownish but faithful valet, or the garrulous narrative of the heroine's *fille-de-chambre*, when rehearsing the stories of blood and horror which she had heard in the servants' hall?" (1: 40)

1815

E99   Austen, Jane. *Emma.* 1815. Bucks, U.K.: Penguin, 1982.

Harriet Smith criticizes Robert Martin for not having read *Romance of the Forest.*

E100   [Hazlitt, William.] Rev. of Burney's *The Wanderer. Edinburgh Review* 24 (1815): 320-38.

Hazlitt's review of *The Wanderer* includes a survey of the English novel. Finds that Radcliffe's "'enchantments drear' and mouldering castles, derived a part of their interest . . . from the supposed tottering state of all old structures at the time . . ." (335). Revised and reprinted with additional remarks about Radcliffe in "On the English Novelists" (1818).

E101   Robinson, Henry Crabb. Journal entries for 1815. *Henry Crabb Robinson on Books and their Writers.* Ed. Edith J. Morley. 3 vols. 1938. AMS Press, 1967. [Partially published earlier as *Diary, Reminiscences, and Correspondence* (1869).]

Entries for 1815 compare Radcliffe and Scott: On 5 March 1815 briefly compares *Waverley* to Radcliffe's works, finding Scott's "sense of the romantic and picturesque in nature is not so delicate nor is his execution so powerful as in Mrs. Radcliffe. But his paintings of men and manners are more valuable" (1: 163). On 15 September 1815 mentions Radcliffe in discussion of *Guy Mannering:* "There are some scenes of terror, hardly inferior to Mrs. Radcliffe's" (1: 173).

E102   Wordsworth, William. Letter 282 to R.P. Gillies. March or April, 1815. *Letters of the Wordsworth Family from 1787 to 1855.*

Ed. William Knight. 3 vols. Boston: Ginn and Company, 1907. 2:57-58.

Wordsworth accuses Sir Walter Scott of the "want of taste which is universal among modern novels of the Radcliffe school . . ." (2:58).

1816

E103 Rev. of C. Colton's *Hypocrisy. Gentleman's Magazine* 86, Pt. 2 (1816): 330-36.

Review quotes lines referring to "Udolpho's turrets, and the forest drear" (334).

1817

E104 Robinson, Henry Crabb. 13 January 1817. *Henry Crabb Robinson on Books and their Writers.* Ed. Edith J. Morley. 3 vols. 1938. AMS Press, 1967. [Partially published earlier as *Diary, Reminiscences, and Correspondence* (1869).]

Mentions that he "read the *Sicilian Romance* with interest and curiosity, though I read it some twenty years ago . . ." (1:202).

E105 Ware, John. Untitled poem delivered before the Phi Beta Kappa Society, Harvard University, 28 August 1817. *North American Review* 6 (1817): 109-115.

Mocks stock conventions of Radcliffe imitators: "The thousand pupils of the Radcliffe school;/ Sprung from a vigorous root, the puny flock/ Bears small resemblance to the parent stock" (111).

1818

E106 Byron, George Gordon, Lord. *Childe Harold's Pilgrimage. Byron.* Ed. Jerome McGann. NY: Oxford UP, 1986. 19-206.

Byron acknowledges Radcliffe's influence in description of Venice, canto 4, verse xviii (published in 1818):

> I lov'd her from my boyhood—she to me
> Was as a fairy city of the heart,
> Rising like water-columns from the sea,
> Of joy the sojourn, and of wealth the mart;

And Otway, Radcliffe, Schiller, and Shakespeare's art,
Had stamp'd her image in me. . . .

E107   Dyce, A. Letter to Mr. Urban. *Gentleman's Magazine* 88, Pt. 1
[ns 10] (1818): 121-22.

Points out Byron's "plagiarisms" (including borrowings from
Udolpho) in *Lara*, "one of his most nervous pieces" (121).

E108   Letter to Mr. Urban signed C.C. *Gentleman's Magazine* 88, Pt.
1 [ns 10] (1818): 390-91.

Attacks Dyce in an attempt to vindicate Byron.

E109   Hazlitt, William. "On the English Novelists." *Lectures on the
English Comic Writers*. 1818. London: Oxford UP, 1907: 138-
74.

Revised version of Hazlitt's 1815 review of Burney's *The Wanderer* with added remarks about Radcliffe. Dislikes Radcliffe's
characterization and her descriptions of scenery, which are
"neither like Salvator nor Claude, nor nature nor art" (165),
but admires her horrific and mysterious effects that make
"her readers twice children" (165).

E110   Keats, John. Letter to John Hamilton Reynolds. 14 March
1818. *Letters of John Keats*. Ed. Frederick Page. London: Oxford UP, 1954. 89-92.

Refers to Radcliffe: ". . . I am going among Scenery whence I
intend to tip you the Damosel Radcliffe—I'll cavern you, and
grotto you, and waterfall you, and wood you, and water you,
and immense-rock you, and tremendous-sound you, and soli-
tude you" (90).

E111   W. "Nugæ Literariæ." *New Monthly Magazine and Universal
Register* 10 (1 November 1818): 293-94.

Conjectures that the veiled picture in *Udolpho* may have been
inspired by an encounter with a similar image in Louvain.

1819

E112   "Estimate of the Literary Character of Mrs. Ann Ratcliffe
[*sic*]." *Monthly Magazine* 47 (1819): 125-26.

Praises Radcliffe as the "greatest sorceress in *the terrific* that
has ever appeared" (125). Radcliffe does not indulge in the

wild improbabilities of Walpole or the exaggerated passions of German literature. Brief comparisons with Shakespeare, Byron, Schiller, Bunyan. In her descriptions of depravity, Radcliffe has "dared to lay open the arteries of *male* dereliction from the oracles of the heart to the marrow in the bones. She has penetrated beyond the metaphysics of her sex, and exposed the criminality peculiar to ours" (126).

E113 Keats, John. Letter to George and Georgiana Keats dated 14 February to 3 May 1819. *Letters of John Keats.* Ed. Frederick Page. London: Oxford UP, 1954. 231-72.

Refers to "mother Radcliffe" (235).

1820

E114 "Sketch of the Progress of Novel-writing." [From the *British Review*] *Port Folio* 9 (1820): 266-86. [Rptd. in "On Novel Writing." *Western Monthly Magazine* 2 (1834): 193-201 and 225-37.]

Survey of the history of the novel contrasts the sentimental and Gothic novel. Response to Radcliffe is mixed: Although Radcliffe was "an extraordinary female, and her style of writing . . . must be allowed to form an era in English romances," she exhibits an "ignorance nearly equal to her imagination, and that is saying a great deal" (275). Nevertheless, finds Radcliffe's romances "irresistibly and dangerously delightful; fitted to inspire a mind devoted to them with a species of melancholy madness" (276). Criticizes imitators.

E115 Stuart, Lady Louisa [a granddaughter of Lady Mary Wortley Montagu]. Letter to Louisa Clinton dated 11 February 1820. *The Letters of Lady Louisa Stuart.* Ed. R. Brimley Johnson. NY: The Dial Press, 1926. 171-77.

Attacks Radcliffe's "most disgusting species of anachronism, the polished manners and sentimental cant of modern times put in the fifteenth and sixteenth centuries. The enlightened philosophy likewise! young ladies arguing with their maids against their belief of ghosts and witches when a judge durst not have expressed his doubts of either upon the bench. This *palavering* style has crept into history through Miss Aitken . . ." (175).

1821

E116   "Literary Intelligence." *Gentleman's Magazine* 91, Pt. 2 (1821): 451.

Discusses the profits of authors. For *Udolpho* Radcliffe received 1,000 pounds, which was considered to be a handsome sum.

1822

E117   J.J. "London Chit-Chat." *Blackwood's Magazine* 11 (1822): 331-34.

Reports that Radcliffe is returning to writing after a long hiatus (331).

1823

E118   Obituary. *Athenaeum* [Boston] 13 (July 1823): 275-76.

Virtually the same as obituary in *New Monthly Magazine.*

E119   Obituary. *Gentleman's Magazine* 93, Pt. 2 (July 1823): 87-88.

Discusses Radcliffe's international reputation as a pioneering English novelist and supreme writer of romance. Characterizes Radcliffe as one of the brightest of "the female ornaments of English literature" (87). Remarks that she was short (!) but, nevertheless, praises her vivacious conversation for being "unalloyed by the pedantic formality which too often characterizes the manners of literary ladies" (88). Although this obituary is briefer, language is similar to *New Monthly Magazine* and *Athenaeum* obituaries.

E120   Obituary. *New Monthly Magazine* ns 9 (May 1823): 232.

Lists editions, translations, profits. Praises *Udolpho.* Comments on the explained supernatural and Radcliffe's mental and physical health. Virtually the same as *Athenaeum* obituary. Expanded version of *Gentleman's Magazine* obituary.

E121   Obituary. *Port Folio* 16 (1823): 137-39.

Similar to obituaries in *New Monthly Magazine* and *Monthly Magazine.*

E122   "The Periodical Press." *Edinburgh Review* 38 (1823): 349-78.

Note mentions Radcliffe's reticence: "The fair authoress kept herself almost as much *incognito* as the Author of Waverley; nothing was known of her but her name in the title page. She never appeared in public, nor mingled in private society, but kept herself apart, like the sweet bird that sings its solitary notes, shrowded and unseen" (360).

1824

E123   Brydges, Egerton. Letter dated 17 July 1824. *Recollections of Foreign Travel, On Life, Literature and Self-Knowledge.* 2 vols. London: Longman, Hurst, Rees, Orme, Brown, and Green, 1825. 1: 34-47.

Placing her in good company, Brydges precipitously points to Radcliffe as passé: "[W]hat novel has outlasted the manners of its age? Who now reads *Fielding, Smollett, Richardson, Mackenzie, Burney, Radcliffe, Charlotte Smith?*" (1: 40).

E124   "Memoirs of Mrs. Radcliffe." Prefixed to *The Mysteries of Udolpho.* London: Printed for J. Limbird, 1824. v-vii.

Short sketch of Radcliffe.

E125   "Memoirs of Miss S. Lee." *Minerva* (New York) ns 1 (1824): 247.

Remarks that Radcliffe, who was acquainted with Sophia Lee's family, greatly admired Lee's *The Recess.*

E126   "Mrs. Ann Radcliffe." *Annual Biography and Obituary for the Year . . . .* 8 (1824): 89-105.

Obituary includes brief biography and extended extracts from Barbauld's prefatory introduction to Radcliffe. Radcliffe was widely praised by her contemporaries including Sheridan, Fox, (Joseph) Warton, and Mathias. Ends with biographical letter from a relative/acquaintance that describes Radcliffe and her family, details an altercation caused by the publication of Seward's letters, includes some trivial correspondence with Mrs. Carter, and discusses her contemporary reputation.

E127   Scott, Sir Walter. "Prefatory Memoir to Mrs. Ann Radcliffe." *The Novels of Mrs. Ann Radcliffe.* Ballantyne's Novelist's Library. Edinburgh: Printed by James Ballantyne; London: Published by Hurst, Robinson, and Co., 1824. 10: i-xxxix.

Influential and frequently cited sketch of Radcliffe's development. In much-quoted words, dubs her "the first poetess of romantic fiction, that is, if actual rythm [*sic*] shall not be deemed essential to poetry" (10: iv). Argues that Radcliffe finds her style in *Romance of the Forest*, where she demonstrates that she has "the eye of a painter, with the spirit of a poet" (10: vi). Discusses the popularity of *The Mysteries of Udolpho*: "The very name was fascinating, and the public, who rushed upon it with all the eagerness of curiosity, rose from it with unsated appetite" (10: vii). Finds *Udolpho* more intense than *Romance of the Forest*. Praises descriptive passages (which approach the style of Claude, Poussin, or Salvator Rosa) in *The Italian* but notes imperfections where Radcliffe "like a careless knitter, neglected to take up her 'loose stitches'" (10: xiv). Although criticizes Radcliffe's stereotypical characters and her explained supernatural, awards her high praise for her innovations: "MRS RADCLIFFE, as an author, has the most decided claim to take her place among the favoured few, who have been distinguished as the founders of a class, or school. She led the way in a peculiar style of composition . . ." (10: xvii).

1825

E128   Dyce, Alexander. *Specimens of British Poetesses.* London: T. Rodd, 1825.

Anthologizes several of Radcliffe's poems.

1826

E129   [Hogg, James?]. "Noctes Ambrosianæ." No. 27. *Blackwood's* 20 (1826): 90-109.

Brief references to Radcliffe.

E130   Scott, Sir Walter. Entry for 3 February 1826. *The Journal of Sir Walter Scott.* Ed. John Guthrie Tait. Edinburgh: Oliver and Boyd, 1950.

A defense against James Ballantyne's accusation that *Woodstock* contained imitations of Radcliffe: "J. B. is severely critical on what he calls imitations of Mrs. Radcliffe in *Woodstock*. Many will think with him—yet I am of opinion he is quite wrong. . . . I am to look on the mere fact of another author having treated a subject happily as a bird looks on a potatoe-bogle which scares it away from a field otherwise as free to its depredations as any one's else!" (87-88)

E131 [Talfourd, Sir Thomas Noon (Serjeant Talfourd). From information supplied by William Radcliffe.] "Memoir of the Life and Writings of Mrs. Radcliffe." Prefixed to *Gaston de Blondeville....* 1826. Intro. Devendra Varma. NY: Arno 1972.

Earliest full biography of Radcliffe from materials apparently supplied by her husband. Includes literary criticism and extracts from Radcliffe's journals. Forms the basis of all future biographies.

REVIEWS AND NOTICES OF *GASTON*...

[See also Dana, 1827 and *Edinburgh Review*, 1834.]

E132 *Blackwood's Magazine* 20 (1826): 113.

Listed.

E133 *Gentleman's Magazine* 96, Pt. 1 (1826): 258.

Advance notice of *Gaston. . . .*

E134 Rev. of *Gaston. . . . Ladies' Monthly Museum* 24 (1826): 45-46.

Negative review finds the novel dull and unoriginal. Observes that, like most posthumous works, this one disappoints: "Mrs. Radcliffe seems to have shewn her judgment in withholding it from publication" (45).

E135 Rev. of *Gaston. . . . Literary Gazette* (London) Nos. 488 and 489 (May and June 1826): 321-23, 346-47.

Considers Radcliffe "the finest writer" of the Gothic "that ever existed" (321). She affected "thousands, over whose imaginations she had ruled with the sway of an enchantress" (321). She is "at the head of her class" (321). Admires her moral precepts, even if they detract from her heroines, who are too prone to tears: "Her prudence . . . does detract a little from the grace of her heroines, with whom we should, moreover, be better pleased if they did not weep so much— the constant habit of which must have made them look old before their time" (321). Prefers Radcliffe's sentimental scenes over her scenes of terror. If the plot and characters of

Gaston are less complicated than those of her other novels, the writing is more refined.

Finds *St. Alban's Abbey* too diffuse and antiquarian. Pronounces the Memoir and the extracts from Radcliffe's journals interesting. Disparages Radcliffe's reticence about being an author.

E136 *Museum of Foreign Literature and Science and Art* ns 1 (1826): 94, 190, 287, 384 and ns 2 (1826): 192-93.

Advance notice of *Gaston*. . . .

E137 Rev. of *Gaston*. . . . *New Monthly Magazine* 16 (1826): 532-36.

High general praise for Radcliffe's works, which have endured. Agrees with Memoir prefixed to *Gaston* that Radcliffe withheld *Gaston* from publication during her lifetime because "The splendour of her own reputation alarmed her feminine apprehensiveness and pride . . ." (533). Disagrees with reports of her insanity. Praises *Gaston*, although it differs considerably from her previous works. Includes plot summary of *Gaston*.

E138 *North American Review* 23 (1826): 503.

Lists American edition.

E139 Rev. of *Gaston*. . . . signed "B." *Scots Magazine* ns 18 (1826): 703-704.

Praises the novel as more concentrated than Radcliffe's previous romances. Applauds her mode of appending the poetry.

4

CRITICISM, 1827–1899 (C)

1827

C1   Rev. of *Almack's* and of *Vivian Grey* in *North American Review* 25 (1827): 183-203.

Takes the occasion of the review to discuss the development of the novel. Compares English literature with that of other countries. Finds contemporary English fiction unburdened by "the licentiousness of Fielding and Smollett, the sentimentality of Burney and Radcliffe, and the painful elaboration of Richardson" (192).

C2   [Dana, Richard Henry.] Rev. of *Gaston*. . . . *United States Review and Literary Gazette* 2 (1827): 1-8.

After a long biographical meditation occasioned by the memoir, finds that *Gaston*, compared to Radcliffe's other works, is an improvement stylistically but lacks energy. The ghost is "a daylight sort of ghost" (6). Praises the extracts from Radcliffe's journals but finds her poetry disappointing.

1829

C3   Robinson, Henry Crabb. Entries for June, 1829. *Henry Crabb Robinson on Books and their Writers*. Ed. Edith J. Morley. 3 vols. 1938. AMS Press, 1967. [Partially published earlier as *Diary, Reminiscences, and Correspondence* (1869).]

On 23 June 1829 Robinson read *Udolpho* "which occupies time that might be better employed. But though not so strongly as in youth, this romance even now is capable of diverting my attention from objects that would seem to be irresistible in their demands . . ." (1: 366).

On 27 June 1829 notes that he has finished reading *Udolpho*, "which I ought not to have begun. Yet towards the end it indisposed me to any other occupation. But, after all, the interest is merely that of the worry of finding out a riddle. The poetry and much of the descriptions I skipped. Yet thirty years ago these were much admired . . ." (1: 366).

C4   Rev. of Sir Walter Scott's *Anne of Geierstein*. *The Examiner* June 14, 1829: 370-71.

Refers to parts of this novel as "Radcliffe redivive" (371).

1830

C5   Macnish, Robert. *The Philosophy of Sleep*. Glasgow: W.R. M'Phun, 1830.

Radcliffe's diet encouraged nightmares: "[F]or the purpose of filling her sleep with those phantoms of horror, which she has so forcibly embodied in the 'Mysteries of Udolpho,' and 'Romance of the Forest,' [Radcliffe] is said to have supped upon the most indigestible substances . . ." (57).

C6   "The Old Story. A 'Psychological Curiosity.'" *New Monthly Magazine* 29 (1830): 87-93.

Brief reference to the "swarm of tenth-rate imitators, which tried to combine the perplexities of Madame D'arblay and the romantic verbiage of Mrs. Radcliffe" (88-89).

1831

C7   "Joanna Baillie." *Museum of Foreign Literature and Science and Art* ns 12 (1831): 282-83. [From *The Athenaeum*.]

Brief mention of Radcliffe: "We have not, and are not likely to have at present, another Mary Wolstencroft [*sic*], . . . another Mrs. Inchbald, another Mrs. Radcliffe—Joanna Baillie is their only representative; adding, to the power of mind which they possessed . . . " (282).

1832

C8   [Prescott, William?] "English Literature of the Nineteenth Century." *North American Review* 35 (1832): 165-95.

Brief reference to Radcliffe: " . . . Mrs. Radcliffe is good for nothing out of it [the picturesque], except, indeed, when she is in her horrors" (188).

1834

C9   Ainsworth, William Harrison. *Rookwood.* 1834. Rptd. in *Historical Romances of William Harrison Ainsworth.* Philadelphia: Printed for subscribers by George Barrie and Sons, n.d.

Preface, which may have been added in 1849, acknowledges that *Rookwood* (1834) was influenced by Radcliffe: ". . . I resolved to attempt a story in the bygone style of Mrs. Radcliffe,—which had always inexpressible charms for me . . . "(xvii).

C10   A Beckett, William, Jr. *A Universal Biography.* 3 vols. 1836. London: G.F. Isaac, [1834?]. 3: 567.

Brief biographical sketch concludes, "As a romance writer, this lady stands at the head of her class, and in some of her literary characteristics, she has been compared to Shakespeare."

C11   Cunningham, Allan. "Anne [*sic*] Radcliffe.' *Biographical and Critical History of the British Literature of the Last 50 Years.* Paris: Baudry's Foreign Library, 1834. 122-25. [Rptd. from *The Athenæum* in *Museum of Foreign Literature and Science and Art* ns 17 (1834): 388-89.]

Allows that Radcliffe had a certain talent, but criticizes her technique of taking in the reader, predicting Radcliffe will not endure. Observes that "we extend not a little of our ill-will to the writer who took such pains to put us out of humour with ourselves" (125).

C12   Rev. of *The Poetical Works of Ann Radcliffe. St Alban's Abbey; a Metrical Romance. With other Poems. Edinburgh Review* 59 (1834): 327-41.

Rptd. in *Museum of Foreign Literature and Science and Art* ns 18 (1834): 438-44.

Reviewer of these poems from *Gaston* objects that they have been previously published. Devotes relatively little space to the poems. Blasts *St Alban's Abbey*: "There seem . . . to be some who are poets in prose, but whose poetry forsakes them the moment they attempt to embody their ideas in verse; and one of these undoubtedly was Mrs Radcliffe" (337). High praise for the originality of Radcliffe's romances and criticism of her imitators. Compares Radcliffe and Clara Reeve. Defends Radcliffe's undiscriminated characters, which allow her to focus on the scene and atmosphere in order to excite fear. Defends the descriptions of landscapes in her novels and praises (and provides extracts of) the descriptions of nature in her journals not meant for publication. Criticizes *Gaston de Blondeville* for its tedious plot and antiquarian descriptions.

1835

C13   Poe, Edgar Allan. "I Promessi Sposi." *Southern Literary Messenger* 1 (1835): 520-22. Rptd. in *The Complete Works of Edgar Allan Poe*. Ed. J.A. Harrison. 17 vols. 1902. NY: AMS, 1965. 8: 12-18.

Brief reference to Radcliffe: "We have had the Ratcliffe [*sic*] dynasty, the Edgeworth dynasty, and the Scott dynasty; each, like the family of the Caesars, passing from good to bad, and from bad to worse, until each has run out" (8: 12).

1836

C14   Rev. of S.G. Goodrich, *The Outcast and Other Poems*. *American Monthly Magazine* 6 (1836): 519-25.

Radcliffe still held up as the standard of comparison: "Mrs. Radcliffe's horrors are cakes and gingerbread to those of Mr. Goodrich" (522).

1837

C15   Bucke, Charles. *On the Beauties, Harmonies, and Sublimities of Nature*. [First published anonymously in 1813 under the title *The Philosophy of Nature*.] New enlarged edn. London: Printed for Thomas Tegg and Son, 1837. 122-23.

The later enlarged edition adds a footnote praising Radcliffe's personal qualities.

C16 Robinson, Henry Crabb. Journal entry for 12 September 1837. *Henry Crabb Robinson on Books and their Writers*. Ed. Edith J. Morley. 3 vols. 1938. AMS Press, 1967. [Partially published earlier as *Diary, Reminiscences, and Correspondence* (1869).] 2: 538.

Briefly mentions Radcliffe.

1839

C17 Hazlitt, William. "Why the Heroes of Romances are Insipid." *Sketches and Essays*. 1839 [posthumously]. London: Oxford UP, 1912. 173-85.

Criticizes Radcliffe's heroes as insipid and indistinguishable: "Her heroes have no character at all" (180).

C18 Moir, George. *Treatises on Poetry, Modern Romance, and Rhetoric; being the Articles under those Heads, Contributed to the Encyclopaedia Britannica, seventh edition*. Edinburgh: Adam & Charles Black, 1839. 197-206.

Praises Radcliffe for her use of suggestive details and her landscape painting, but finds fault with her explained supernatural and interspersed verses. Radcliffe's characterization is slight, subordinate to the creation of curiosity. Although Schedoni is the most fully elaborated character, he is inconsistent. *The Castles of Athlin and Dunbayne* and *A Sicilian Romance* are "wholly and deservedly forgotten" (203), while *Udolpho* is generally considered to be her best work. Praises section dealing with the disappearance of Ludovico. Suggests that Radcliffe's novels are best read in youth.

C19 Rev. of *Stanley, or the Recollections of a Man of the World. New York Review* 4 (1839): 237-39.

Reviewer finds *Stanley* "full of strange Castle-of-Udolpho scenes . . ." (238).

1840

C20 Thackeray, William Makepeace. *A Shabby Genteel Story. The Adventures of Philip . . . to which is prefixed A Shabby Genteel Story*. Introd. Anne Thackeray Ritchie. 1840. NY: Harper and Brothers, 1899.

Readers are asked, "Had Caroline read of Valancourt and Emily for nothing . . . ?" (47)

1841

C21   Pushkin, Alexander. *Dubrovsky. The Captain's Daughter and
           Other Tales.* Trans. and Introd. Natalie Duddington. 1841.
           NY: Dutton, 1965. 147-216.

Brief reference indicates familiarity with Radcliffe in nineteenth-century Russia: Marya Kirilovna was "nourished on
the mysterious horrors of Mrs. Radcliffe" (183).

1842

C22   Poe, Edgar Allan. "The Oval Portrait." *Graham's Magazine,*
           April, 1842; *Broadway Journal* 1: 17. Rptd. in *The Complete
           Works of Edgar Allan Poe.* Ed. James A. Harrison. NY: AMS
           Press, 1965. Vol. 4 [Tales, vol. 3]: 245.

Brief reference to Radcliffe: "The chateau . . . was one of
those piles of commingled gloom and grandeur which have
so long frowned among the Apennines, not less in fact than
in the fancy of Mrs. Radcliffe."

C23   Sand, George. *Consuelo.* 1842-43. Trans. Francis G. Shaw. 3
           vols. NY: William H. Graham, 1846.

Compares narrator to Radcliffe: "If the ingenious and fruit-
ful Anne [*sic*] Radcliffe had been in the place of the candid
and unskilful narrator of this veracious history, she would
not have permitted to escape so good an opportunity of
leading you, lady reader, through corridors, trap doors, spi-
ral staircases and subterranean darkness, during half a dozen
beautiful and attractive volumes, to reveal to you only at the
seventh all the arcana of her learned work" (1: 271).

C24   Talfourd, T. Noon (Serjeant Talfourd). "On British Novels
           and Romances, Introductory to a Series of Criticisms on the
           Living Novelists." *Critical and Miscellaneous Writings of T. Noon
           Talfourd.* Vol. 7 of *The Modern British Essayists.* 1842. Philadel-
           phia: A. Hart, 1852. 7: 5-8. [*New Monthly Magazine.*]

Essay ends with a brief appreciation of Radcliffe's "wild and
wondrous tales" (8), arguing, "Of all romance writers Mrs.
Radcliffe is the most romantic." Regrets her "impotent" conclusions (8).

C25   Thackeray, William Makepeace. Letter to Mrs. Carmichael-
           Smyth. June, 1842. *The Letters and Private Papers of William*

Makepeace Thackeray. Ed. Gordon N. Ray. 4 vols. Cambridge, MA: Harvard UP, 1945. 2: 51-55.

Refers to getting *The Italian* from a library.

1843

C26 Carlyle, Thomas. *Past and Present.* In *Past and Present, Chartism, and Sartor Resartus.* 1843. NY: Harper and Brothers, n.d.

Mentions Radcliffe (42).

C27 Elwood, Anne Katharine (Curteis). "Mrs. Radcliffe." *Memoirs of the Literary Ladies of England, from the Commencement of the Last Century.* 2 vols. London: Henry Colburn, 1843. 2: 155-73.

Flattering account of Radcliffe's career. *Romance of the Forest* established her reputation, while *Udolpho* gained the most popularity. This novel "had the singular merit of interesting not only the very young, and those who seek only for amusement when they read, but of attracting the admiration of men of wit and talent" (2: 158) such as Fox, Sheridan, (Joseph) Warton, Mathias, and Scott. *The Italian,* though not as popular with the common reader as *Udolpho* or *Romance of the Forest,* "was considered as equal, and, by some, superior, to its predecessors" (2: 160-61). Appreciates Radcliffe's descriptions.

1844

C28 Chambers, Robert, ed. "Ann Radcliffe." *Cyclopædia of English Literature.* 2 vols. Edinburgh: William and Robert Chambers, 1844. 2: 554-58.

Praises Radcliffe's descriptions, dubbing her "the Salvator Rosa of British novelists" (2: 554). Criticizes her explained supernatural: "It is as if some theatrical artist were to display to his audience the coarse and mean materials by which his brilliant stage effects were produced, instead of leaving undisturbed the strong impressions they have produced on the imagination" (2: 556). Finds Radcliffe's verse "less truly poetical than her prose" (2: 554). Faults her for lack of character development. Seems unaware of *Gaston de Blondeville.* Includes excerpts.

1845

C29   Alison, Archibald. "The Historical Romance." 1845. [First published in *Blackwood's Magazine.*] *Essays.* 3 vols. Edinburgh and London: William Blackwood and Sons, 1850. 3: 521-50.

Brief reference to Radcliffe's novels as "now wellnigh unreadable" (3: 529).

C30   Wade, Robert L. "The Circulating Library." *Columbian Magazine* 4 (1845): 87-90.

Observations on examining the catalogue of a circulating library. Compares the taste of the eighteenth- and nineteenth-century reading public: "Whole armies of readers have abandoned to their fate the highly wrought scenes and supernatural incidents of Mrs. Radcliffe and Monk Lewis, to breathe a purer atmosphere in the dominions of more rational novelists. . . . [I]n fact all the robbers and murders of the Radcliffian dynasty, have lost their occupation . . ." (88). Contrasts Radcliffe and Scott. Although Wade is perplexed by the eighteenth-century enthusiasm for the supernatural or "that taste that loved to sup so full of horrors" (89), he finds Radcliffe's explained supernatural "very considerate on the part of the lady author" (89).

1847

C31   Hunt, Leigh. *Men, Women, and Books.* 1847. London: Smith, Elder, and Co., 1876.

Brief reference to Radcliffe's verses as being unworthy of her novels. For Mathias, Radcliffe is "a mighty magician," but for Hunt, at least in her poetry, "she is a tinselled nymph in a pantomime, calling up commonplaces with a wand" (278).

1848

C32   "Hints to Novelists." *John-Donkey* 1 (1848): 11-12.

Describes Radcliffe as an example of the "high pressure highfaluting style" because she "presented her readers with a confused array of ruined castles, secret panels, mysterious phantoms, sheeted ghosts, gloomy monks, daggers, poison, groans, shrieks, growls and grunts" (11).

C33   Rose, Hugh James. "RADCLIFFE, (Ann)." *A New General Bio-*

graphical Dictionary. 12 vols. 1848. London: T. Fellowes et al., 1857. 11: 275.

Brief biographical consideration.

C34   Rowton, Frederic, ed. *The Female Poets of Great Britain*. London: Longman, Brown, Green, and Longmans, 1848.

Includes brief introduction to Radcliffe's anthologized poems, "To the Wind," "The Glow-Worm," and "Song of a Spirit."

1849

C35   Brontë, Charlotte. *Shirley*. 1849. Oxford: The Clarendon Press, 1979.

Caroline Helstone and Rose Yorke discuss *The Italian*, which Caroline feels ends in "disappointment, vanity, and vexation of spirit" (452).

C36   Hunt, Leigh. Introduction to "Ludovico in the Haunted Chamber." *A Book for a Corner*. 1849. NY: H.W. Derby, 1861.

Introduction to extract from *Udolpho* prefers Radcliffe to Walpole. Appreciates Radcliffe's explained supernatural and her descriptions.

C37   Mitford, Mary Russell. Letter to Charles Boner dated 6 May 1849. *Correspondence with Charles Boner and John Ruskin*. Ed. Elizabeth Lee. 1914. Chicago: Rand McNally, 1915.

Comments on Radcliffe's reputation in France: "It is quite amusing to see how much a writer, wellnigh forgotten in England, is admired in France. . . . [S]uch critics as Ste.-Beuve, such poets as Victor Hugo, such novelists as Balzac and George Sand, to say nothing of a thousand inferior writers, talk of her in raptures. I will venture to say that she is quoted fifty times where Scott is quoted once" (134-35).

C38   Paulding, J. K. *The Puritan and his Daughter*. 3 vols. NY: Baker and Scribner, 1849.

Brief reference to Radcliffe: "The most racy book I ever read was an abridgement of the Romances of Mrs. Radcliffe and some others, in which all the connecting links were left out, and nothing retained but the incidents" (1: 109).

1850

C39   "The Editor's Table." *Knickerbocker* 35 (February 1850): 179.

A "clever correspondent" remembers his school days spent poring over *Udolpho* until his hair stood on end.

1851

C40   Arvine, Kazlitt. *The Cyclopædia of Anecdotes of Literature and the Fine Arts.* Boston: Gould and Lincoln, 1851. 268-70.

Briefly describes the Radcliffes' domestic life. Relates annecdote of Davies' attempt to publish spurious posthumous work (actually by Robert Will) while Radcliffe was still alive.

C41   Moir, D.M. Lecture I. *Sketches of the Poetical Literature of the Past Half-Century.* 1851. Edinburgh and London: William Blackwood and Sons, 1852. 1-58.

Walpole's success "taught Mrs. Radcliffe and others to harp— and far from unpleasantly—on the same string. 'Clarissa Harlowe' and 'Pamela,' quietly located on the book-shelves, had for a while their 'virtue unrewarded,' even by a reading; and nothing went down but 'Udolphos' and 'Romances of the Forest' . . ." (18).

1852

C42   "Anecdote of Mrs. Radcliffe." *Godey's Magazine* 45 (1852): 225-27.

Odd parody has Radcliffe wrongly imprisoned in France in 1795. Here she has nightly spectral visitations, the result of "a partial disarrangement of the nervous system" (227). Although Radcliffe's romances were popular in her day, they now appear to be "the efflux of a morbid imagination, full of hallucinations and absurdities, and insufferably tedious to our modern tastes . . ." (227).

1853

C43   Thackeray, William Makepeace. *The Newcomes.* Published in numbers, 1853-55. NY: Harper & Brothers, 1898.

Brief reference to Radcliffe (293-94).

1854

C44 "Novels: Their Meaning and Mission." *Putnam's Monthly* 4 (1854): 389-96.

Brief reference to Radcliffe classifies her works as "*Extrava-ganzas*" and "*bizarreries*" (394).

C45 Sand, George. *Histoire de ma vie.* 1854-55. Translated as *Convent Life of George Sand.* Trans. Maria Ellery MacKaye. Boston: Roberts Brothers, 1893.

Influence of Radcliffe on schoolgirl Gothic adventures (37, 39).

1855

C46 Allibone, Samuel Austin. "Radcliffe, Anne [*sic*]." *A Critical Dictionary of English Literature and British and American Authors Living and Deceased.* 1855. 3 vols. Philadelphia: Lippincott, 1897. 2: 1721-22.

Entry consists mostly of quoted responses to Radcliffe. Observes ". . . surely there is enough to satisfy the taste for fiction . . . without resorting to the assassins, the libertines, the haunted castles, and the horrid dungeons of Radcliffe, of Lewis, of Maturin, and of Godwin!" (1721)

1857

C47 Trollope, Anthony. *Barchester Towers.* 1857. 2 vols.   London: Geoffrey Cumberlege, Oxford UP, 1953.

Brief reference to Radcliffe: "When we have once learnt what was that picture before which was hung Mrs. Ratcliffe's [*sic*] solemn curtain, we feel no further interest about either the frame or the veil. They are to us, merely a receptacle for old bones, an inappropriate coffin, which we would wish to have decently buried out of our sight" (1: 143).

1858

C48 Rev. of *Guy Livingstone. Knickerbocker* 51 (1858): 73-77.

Brief reference: "As the heroines of the Radcliffe school of romances say: 'I turned to thank my preserver—but he was gone'" (74).

C49   Jeaffreson, J. Cordy. "Ann Radcliffe." *Novels and Novelists from Elizabeth to Victoria.* 2 vols. London: Hurst & Blackett, 1858. 2: 1-6.

Begins with short biographical sketch, observing, "Like many, and perhaps we may add *the best* of our female writers, Mrs. Radcliffe passed a retired life . . ." (2:1). Finds that although contemporaries continue to read and remember Radcliffe's works, these novels are unjustly scorned. Defends Radcliffe as the first to "adorn" the novel with descriptions of scenery (4). Criticizes Radcliffe's poetry. Ignores *Gaston.*

C50   Reviewed negatively in *The Athenaeum* (London) 2 (1858): 134.

C51   Rev. of *Rita, an Autobiography. The Athenaeum* (London) 2 (1858): 321-22.

Reference to Radcliffe compares her explained supernatural (viewed as compassionate) to imitations, which were far more violent.

1859

C52   "A Romance of the Old School." *Bentley's Miscellany* 46 (1859): 573-79.

In passing considers George Sand's *L'Homme de Neige* as an imitation of "the thrilling romances" (573) of Radcliffe.

1862

C53   Kavanagh, Julia. *English Women of Letters: Biographical Sketches.* 2 vols. 1862. London: Hurst and Blackett, 1863. 1: 235-331.

Begins with brief biographical discussion. Kavanagh is amazed that Radcliffe never corrected reports issued during her life-time that she was dead or insane. Laments lack of education for women. Considers Radcliffe "the foundress of a new school, not a good one, it may be, but one so fertile in interest and beauty, spite its faults, that more than two generations have not yet exhausted its abundant stores" (242). At this distance in time, finds that Radcliffe is hardly read. Although appreciates Radcliffe's scenery, outlines defects of Radcliffe's novels, insisting that "her characters were an almost total failure" (1: 308). Includes much plot summary.

1863

C54 Palmer, A.H., ed. Letter #32 to Laura Richmond [1863]. *The Life and Letters of Samuel Palmer*. London: Seeley, 1892. 248-50. [Reviewed in 1892.]

Refers to a painting that "enraptured dear Mother Radcliffe" (249). Radcliffe's landscape descriptions are better than Scott's.

1864

C55 "Dying a Natural Death." *Sharpe's London Magazine* ns 25 (1864): 260-263.

Article signed T.F.D.C. asks whether the reader finds the title of the present article as "mysterious as 'Udolpho'" (260).

C56 Knight, Charles. *Passages from a Working Life*. 3 vols. London: Bradbury and Evans, 1864-65. (Vol. 1, 1864). 1: 221.

Brief reference to Radcliffe in description of society around 1820: "Novel-reading was general. Miss Porter and Miss Edgeworth and Mrs. Radcliffe still held their ancient empire, and were not driven out by the Waverley Novels."

C57 Le Fanu, Joseph Sheridan. *Uncle Silas: A Tale of Bartram-Haugh*. Intro. Elizabeth Bowen. 1864. London: Cresset Press, 1947.

Architecture compared to Radcliffe: "It was plainly one of those great structures in which you might easily lose yourself, and with a pleasing terror it reminded me of that delightful old abbey in Mrs. Radcliffe's romance, among whose silent staircases, dim passages, and long suites of lordly, but forsaken chambers, begirt without by the sombre forest, the family of La Mote [*sic*] secured a gloomy asylum" (236). Maud Ruthyn is compared with Adelaide in *Romance of the Forest*.

1877

C58 Murch, Jerom. "Mrs. Radcliffe." *Mrs. Barbauld and her Contemporaries: Sketches of Some Eminent Literary and Scientific Englishwomen*. London: Longmans, Green and Co., 1877. 138-45.

Acknowledges Radcliffe's "rare intellectual power" (139), but accuses her of lowering the public taste.

1882

C59   Oliphant, Margaret. *The Literary History of England in the End of the Eighteenth and Beginning of the 19th Century.* 3 vols. London: Macmillan, 1882. 2: 277-85.

High praise for Radcliffe's descriptions. Finds her characters old fashioned.

1883

C60   Rossetti, Christina. Letters to William Rossetti dated 1883. *The Family Letters of Christina Georgina Rossetti.* Ed. William Michael Rossetti. NY: Charles Scribner's Sons, 1908.   126-130.

29 June 1883: Laments lack of material about Radcliffe, which eventually caused Rossetti to abandon her projected biography for the *Eminent Women* series: "Mr. Jeaffreson is not encouraging: I am belabouring poor Ingram, and between us all nothing whatsoever have I done. I *Radcliffized* the other day at the Museum, and perceive that the best resource is Talfourd after all, unless it be a *quotation* made by Walter Scott. I doubt if the Memoir is feasible . . . "(126-27).

23 July 1883: Responses to her letter to the *Athenaeum* requesting information on Radcliffe were few. "[A]ll told, I doubt if bulk will anyhow suffice. At present Mr. Ingram and I alike are observing a dignified silence" (130).

1884

C61   Derby, J. C. *Fifty Years Among Authors, Books, and Publishers.* NY: G.W. Carleton, 1884.

Brief reference to Radcliffe's works being published by Derby and Jackson (34).

C62   James, Henry. "George Sand." *French Poets and Novelists.* London: Macmillan, 1884. 149-85.

Negative reference to Radcliffe: " 'Realism' had been invented, or rather propagated; and in the light of *Madame Bovary* her [Sand's] own facile fictions began to be regarded as the work of a sort of superior Mrs. Radcliffe. She was antiquated; she belonged to the infancy of art" (168).

C63   Payn, James. *Some Literary Recollections.* NY: Harper, 1884. [From *Cornhill Magazine.*]

As a boy, Payn preferred reading *Udolpho* to hunting: "Twice a week I had to go hunting; this I abhored. I . . . could ride well enough; but the proceedings were too protracted for my taste, and I wanted to be at home to finish the 'Mysteries of Udolpho' by the fire" (13-14).

1887

C64   Brandl, Alois. *Samuel Taylor Coleridge and the English Romantic School.* English edn. translated with the assistance of the author by Lady Elizabeth Eastlake. London: John Murray, 1887. [First published in Berlin in 1886.]

Argues that *Romance of the Forest* and *Udolpho* were sources for *Christabel.*

1891

C65   Saintsbury, George. Introduction. *Tales of Mystery.* Ed. George Saintsbury. NY: Macmillan, 1891. xiv-xvii.

Includes selections from Radcliffe, Lewis, Maturin. Introduction to excerpts from Radcliffe's novels refers to her as "the acknowledged queen" (xi) of the Gothic. Radcliffe's novels all focus on the adventures of an injured, innocent heroine. In general, Gothics were a reaction against "'correctness' and limitation, part of the effort to recover poetry and romance . . ." (x-xi). Praises *Northanger Abbey*, which depends on *The Romance of the Forest* for its horrors. Objects to exaggerations of her imitators, concluding that Radcliffe was "the mother . . . of a deplorable and, though her own work is spotless, in many cases a rather disreputable family" (xiv).

1892

C66   Rev. of A.H. Palmer, *The Life and Letters of Samuel Palmer, Painter and Etcher. Athenæum* No. 3362 (1892): 441-42.

Briefly refers to the influence of painters on Radcliffe.

1893

C67   Phelps, William Lyon. *The Beginnings of the English Romantic*

Movement: A Study in Eighteenth-Century Literature. 1893. Boston: Ginn, 1904.

Influence of *Otranto* on Radcliffe.

1894

C68   Minto, William. *The Literature of the Georgian Era.* Ed. William Knight. Edinburgh and London: William Blackwood and Sons, 1894.

Defends Radcliffe's explained supernatural. Finds criticisms of this method "an affectation, unless when it comes from a convinced believer in ghosts" (109).

C69   Raleigh, Sir Walter Alexander. *The English Novel.* NY: Charles Scribner's Sons, 1894.

Praises Radcliffe for her scenery and for her influence (especially on Byron). Accords her "a foremost place among the earlier apostles of Romanticism" (227). Ironically credits her with inventiveness: "There is nothing in her books that she did not create" (228) since she had little knowledge of human character or of the countries she described. ("Her ignorance of the world at the time when she wrote was complete and many-sided" 228.) Criticizes her plots, her anachronisms, and her explained supernatural: "[T]he reader is almost ashamed of his terrors when he is confronted with the dull mechanic who has simulated a lion so marvellously" (228).

C70   Ritchie, Anne Thackeray. *Chapters from Some Unwritten Memoirs.* 1894. NY: Harper and Brothers, 1895.

Brief reference to *Udolpho* (6).

1895

C71   Le Fèvre-Deumier, Jules. *Célébrités anglais.* Paris: Firmin-Didot & cie, 1895.

Biographical and critical considerations of James Thomson, Ann Radcliffe, George Psalmanazar, Letitia Elizabeth Landon, and Christopher North (John Wilson).

1896

C72   Garnett, Richard. "Radcliffe, Ann." *Dictionary of National Bi-*

ography. Ed. Sidney Lee. 1896. London: Oxford UP, 1921-22. 16: 563-64.

Biographical consideration of Radcliffe points to the popularity of *Udolpho. The Italian* is usually considered Radcliffe's finest novel. Argues that reports of her insanity were false: "Mrs. Radcliffe appears to have possessed a cheerful and equable temper, and to have manifested no peculiarity except the sensitive aversion to notice which she shared with many other authoresses" (564). Although she is hardly read, and has been surpassed in depicting the explained supernatural by Brockden Brown and Poe, she deserves a position in the history of English literature due to "the founder of a school who was also its most eminent representative" (16: 564). Praises her landscape descriptions but finds that, with the exception of Schedoni, her characters lack human interest.

C73 Saintsbury, George. *A History of Nineteenth-Century Literature.* NY and London: Macmillan, 1896.

Discusses Radcliffe's popularity; positions Lewis as a direct imitator of her work.

1897

C74 Sharp, R. Farquharson. *A Dictionary of English Authors.* 1897. 3rd ed. London: George Redway, n.d. 235.

Brief biographical entry.

1899

C75 Beers, Henry A. *A History of English Romanticism in the Eighteenth Century.* NY: Henry Holt, 1899.

Generally unsympathetic to Radcliffe, Beers complains that her novels are too long, too similar, too sentimental, and too descriptive. Objects to improbabilities in the plot and to romantic commonplaces. Finds characters too conventional. The sentimental heroines, "beset with a thousand difficulties" (252), have a resilience that preserves their sense of decorum. Radcliffe unites romanticism with sentimentalism to bathetic effect. Prefers descriptions in her travel writing to the melodramatic scenery of her novels. Credits Radcliffe with producing terror through mystery. Compares Radcliffe's works with *Otranto* and with the Waverley novels. Discusses her popularity and her influence on Byron, Hazlitt, and Coleridge, among others. Considers *Northanger Abbey*.

C76   Cross, Wilbur. *The Development of the English Novel.* NY: Macmillan, 1899.

Considers *Udolpho* and *The Italian* Radcliffe's best novels. The cause of fear is less artificial in *The Italian*. Radcliffe's heroines and tyrants are conventional. Finds in Radcliffe "the most complete expression of romanticism in English fiction before Scott" (104). Discusses Radcliffe's impact on writers from Maturin to Poe and Hawthorne and considers place of Gothic in history of the novel. Radcliffe was influenced by realism, conveying "the tyrant, the disobedient child, and the detested lover from Harlowe Place to a castle" (108).

5

TWENTIETH-CENTURY CRITICISM, PART I: 1900–1949 (T)

1900

T1   Lang, Andrew. "Mrs. Radcliffe's Novels." *Cornhill Magazine* ns 9 (1900): 23-34. [Same as *The Living Age* 226 (1900): 275-83.]

Radcliffe "paved the way" for Scott, Austen, Byron, Maturin, and Lewis, among others. Prefers *Romance of the Forest* to *Udolpho*. Considers *The Italian* the "roof and crown of Mrs. Radcliffe's work" (32).

T2   Rose, D. Murray. Introduction. *The Mysteries of Udolpho*. London: George Routledge and Sons, n.d., after 1899?

Brief general introduction.

1901

T3   Howells, William Dean. *Heroines of Fiction*. 2 vols. NY and London: Harper and Brothers Publishers, 1901. 1: 83-89.

Calls Radcliffe a "mistress of the art of suspense" (1: 87). Considers (mostly by excerpts and plot summaries of *Udolpho* and *Romance of the Forest*) Radcliffe's heroines. Although their virtue is beyond reproach, they "are apt to fall senseless, when it would be more convenient for them to command themselves. . . . Sometimes they are rather hard of hearing when common-sense speaks . . ." (1: 84). Radcliffe's works survive "to touch or appall the reader . . ." (1: 83).

1902

T4   "Ann Ward Radcliffe." *The Library of Literary Criticism of English and American Authors.* Ed. Charles Wells Moulton. 1902. Gloucester, MA: Peter Smith, 1959. 4: 717-721.

A pastiche of quotations about Radcliffe.

T5   Freye, Walter. *The Influence of Gothic Literature on Sir Walter Scott.* Rostock: H. Winterberg's Buchdruckerei, 1902.

Published version of dissertation shows influence of Coleridge, Lewis, Walpole, and Radcliffe on Scott by quoting parallel passages.

T6   Möbius, Hans. *The Gothic Romance.* Leipzig: Buchdruckerei Grimme & Trömel, 1902.

Published version of dissertation considers (mostly by offering plot summaries) Smollett, Walpole, Reeve, and Radcliffe.

1904

T7   Rose, D. Murray. Introduction. *The Romance of the Forest.* London: George Routledge and Sons; NY: E.P. Dutton, 1904. iii-ix.

Brief general introduction.

1906

T8   Loliée, Frédéric. *A Short History of Comparative Literature from the Earliest Times to the Present Day.* Trans. of *Histoire des littératures comparées* (1903) by M. Douglas Power. NY: G.P. Putnam's Sons; London: Hodder and Stoughton, 1906.

Notes that from 1789 to 1814 fourteen of the acclaimed romance writers were female. Three of these writers "won European reputation, namely, Anne [*sic*] Radcliffe, Maria Edgeworth, and Jane Austen, but especially the two former" (226n).

1907

T9   Coleridge, Ernest Hartley, ed. *Christabel.* London: Henry Frowde (Published under the direction of the Royal Society of Literature), 1907.

". . . I doubt if Coleridge 'conveyed' anything worth mentioning from such contemporary works as . . . Mrs. Radcliffe's *Romance of the Forest.* . . ."

1908

T10 Thorndike, Ashley. *Tragedy.* Boston and NY: Houghton Mifflin, 1908.

Briefly considers Radcliffe's influence.

1909

T11 Meyer, Georges. "Les Romans de Mrs. Radcliffe." *Revue Germanique* 5 (1909): 509-550.

Critique of Radcliffe's novels considers the influence of Patrick Brydone, Henry Swinburne, Hester Lynch Piozzi (Mrs. Thrale), and William Gilpin on Radcliffe and discusses Radcliffe's influence.

T12 Reynolds, Myra. *The Treatment of Nature in English Poetry: Between Pope and Wordsworth.* Chicago: U of Chicago P, 1909.

Appreciates romantic landscape in Radcliffe, who was innovative in her descriptions of the ocean.

1910

T13 Whitmore, Clara H. *Woman's Work in English Fiction: From the Restoration to the Mid-Victorian Period.* NY: Knickerbocker Press, 1910.

Radcliffe excels in her descriptions of the natural and the supernatural. Her heroes and heroines (women of sensibility) are all educated and refined. Her servants provide comic relief, while her villains combine good and evil to stimulate both sympathy and horror. Discusses Radcliffe's influence on Scott.

1911

T14 Harrison, Lucy. "Ann Radcliffe-Novelist." *A Lover of Books: The Life and Literary Papers of Lucy Harrison.* Ed. Amy Greener. NY: Dutton, 1916. 183-204. [The Radcliffe essay was written in 1911.]

Voices many common sentiments: Praises Radcliffe's pioneering poetic descriptions of scenery and architecture and her creation of fear and suspense. Criticizes Radcliffe's explanations of the supernatural for taking "away with one hand what she has given with the other" (188). Bashes her verse: "Her prose may be poetic, but her poetry is certainly prosaic" (189). Criticizes her anachronisms, her lack of humour, and her heroes. Although Radcliffe's heroines are all conventionally beautiful and full of sensibility, they have high moral standards and maintain their independence in romantic relationships: "They do not look for guidance and moral instruction from their lovers . . . nor do they, because they are in love, become passive instruments of the will of another, and abandon their right of independent judgment and action" (195). Praises her villains, especially Schedoni, her "masterpiece" (198). Considers *The Italian* Radcliffe's best work.

1914

T15   Buyers, Geoffrey. "The Influence of Schiller's Drama and Fiction upon English Literature in the Period 1780-1830." *Englische Studien* 48 (1914-15): 349-93.

Includes discussion of influence of *The Ghostseer* on *The Italian*.

1915

T16   Killen, Alice Mary. *Le Roman terrifiant ou roman noir de Walpole à Anne Radcliffe et son influence sur la littérature française jusqu'en 1840.* Paris: G. Cres, 1915.

Pioneering study of Walpole, Reeve, Radcliffe, and Lewis considers their influence on French literature.

1917

T17   Scarborough, Dorothy. *The Supernatural in Modern English Fiction.* NY: G.P. Putnam's Sons, 1917.

One of the first studies of Gothic elements in Radcliffe, among other writers. Studies gloomy architecture, imagined ghosts, mysterious manuscripts, dread secrets, and inexplicable music. Attributes Radcliffe's literary endeavors to the fact that ". . . she had time that was wasting on her hands . . ." (16). Concludes with discussion of *Northanger Abbey*.

T18 Reviewed by Virginia Woolf in *TLS*, January 31, 1918, p. 288.

T19 Summers, Montague. "A Great Mistress of Romance: Ann Radcliffe, 1764-1823." *Essays in Petto.* 1917 [delivered as a lecture]. Freeport, NY: Books for Libraries Press, 1967. 3-29.

Consideration of Radcliffe as a major "power" in English literature. Discusses influences on Radcliffe and her impact on Continental writers. Includes remarks on Walpole, the Shelleys, Reeve, Austen, Maturin, and Godwin.

T20 Rev. of *Essays in Petto. TLS* 26 (April 1928): 312.

Negative review faults Summers for failing to recognize Radcliffe's influence on Coleridge's "Christabel" and on Keats's "Eve of Saint Agnes," which are "of the Udolpho family." Also criticizes Summers for ignoring in Radcliffe's poetry "that delicacy of melody not infrequent among women poets of that day. . . ."

1919

T21 Johnson, Reginald Brimley. *The Women Novelists.* 1919. Freeport, NY: Books for Libraries Press, 1967.

Despite Radcliffe's use of the explained supernatural, she "allows her imagination to wander freely over the realms of superstitious alarm, wherein the *reason* of woman cannot presumably hold sway" (57). Disagrees with the emphasis critics place on mystery. Finds Radcliffe's heroines are "addicted to sensibility" (21).

1921

T22 Birkhead, Edith. "'The Novel of Suspense.' Mrs. Radcliffe." *The Tale of Terror: A Study of the Gothic Romance.* London: Constable, 1921. 38-62.

Pioneering study argues that Radcliffe, who "saved the Gothic tale from an early death," pays little attention to style but emphasizes situation. Discusses her development from romance to suspense in the later novels. Like Lucy Harrison (in 1911), characterizes Schedoni in *The Italian* as Radcliffe's "masterpiece."

T23   Woolf, Virginia. "Gothic Romance" [Review of Edith
Birkhead's *The Tale of Terror*]. *TLS* May 5, 1921: 288.

Woolf wishes that Birkhead had considered "the aesthetic value
of shock and terror and had ventured some analysis of the taste
which demands this particular stimulus" (57).

T24   McIntyre, Clara. "Were the 'Gothic Novels' Gothic?" *PMLA* 36
(1921): 644-67.

Elizabethan influences on Radcliffe.

T25   Shackford, Martha Hale. "*The Eve of St. Agnes* and *The Mysteries of
Udolpho.*" *PMLA* 36 (1921): 104-118.

Influence of *Udolpho* on Keats.

1923

T26   Clyne, Anthony. "Ann Radcliffe, Romancer." *Living Age* 317
(1923): 49-51. [From the *Daily Telegraph.*]

The centenary of Radcliffe's death provides the occasion for
an appreciation.

T27   Ellis, Stewart Marsh. "Ann Radcliffe and her Literary Influence." *Contemporary Review* 123 (1923): 188-97.

Discusses Radcliffe's influence, praises her scenery, criticizes
her explained supernatural.

T28   Ellis, Stewart Marsh. "The Ghost Story and its Exponents."
Originally published in *Fortnightly Review* 120 (1923): 517-27.
Reprinted in his *Mainly Victorian*. 1925. Freeport, NY: Books
for Libraries Press, 1969. 322-31.

Brief consideration of Radcliffe calls her explained supernatural "the great blot" on her artistry: "She trifled with the
supernatural. She summoned spirits from the vasty deep,
and then, alarmed by her own temerity, she dismissed her
potential spectres and substituted puppets and unsatisfactory
explanations" (323).

1924

T29   Moesch, Vasil. *Naturschau und Naturgefühl in den Romanen der*

Mrs. Radcliffe und in der zeitgenössischen englischen Reiseliteratur. Freiburg: Caritas-Druckerei, 1924.

Analysis of nature in Radcliffe and in contemporary English travel writing.

T30 Peck, W.E. "Keats, Shelley, and Mrs. Radcliffe." *Modern Language Notes* 39 (1924): 251-52.

Influence of *Udolpho* on "Ode to a Nightingale" and on *St. Irvyne or the Rosicrucian.*

1925

T31 Birkhead, Edith. "Sentiment and Sensibility in the Eighteenth-Century Novel." *Essays by Members of the English Association.* Vol. 11. Ed. Oliver Elton. Oxford: Clarendon Press, 1925. 92-116.

Scattered references to Radcliffe.

T32 McIntyre, Clara. "The Later Career of the Elizabethan Villain-Hero." *PMLA* 40 (1925): 874-80.

Finds Radcliffe responsible for reviving Elizabethan villains.

T33 Manwaring, Elizabeth Wheeler. *Italian Landscape in Eighteenth Century England: A Study Chiefly of the Influence of Claude Lorrain and Salvator Rosa on English Taste 1700-1800.* NY: Oxford UP, 1925.

Considers the influence of Italian landscape painters on Thomson, Dyer, Kent, Shenstone, and Radcliffe. Radcliffe's scenery was admired by contemporaries despite the occassional complaint about excessive descriptions. With the exception of the posthumous *Gaston de Blondeville*, Radcliffe's landscapes became more elaborate and numerous as she developed. Claude and Salvator, rather than nature, were her models.

T34 Thompson, L.F. "Ann Radcliffe's Knowledge of German." *Modern Language Review* 20 (1925): 190-191.

Argues that before the publication of *Udolpho*, Radcliffe (directly or via her husband) had knowledge of Schiller's *Der Geisterseher* in the original.

1927

T35   Foster, James R. "The Abbé Prevost and the English Novel."
            PMLA 42 (1927): 443-64.

            Includes some discussion of Radcliffe's indebtedness to
            Prevost, either first hand, or through such imitators as Sophia
            Lee and Charlotte Smith. Radcliffe represents "a degraded
            stage of Prevost" (461).

T36   Lovecraft, Howard Phillips. *Supernatural Horror in Literature.*
            1927 [First published in ephemeral magazine; subsequently
            revised.] NY: Dover Publications, 1973.

            Briefly considers Radcliffe.

T37   Railo, Eino. *The Haunted Castle: A Study of the Elements of
            English Romanticism.* London: G. Routlege & Sons; NY: E.P.
            Dutton, 1927.

            References to Radcliffe pepper this exhaustive study of the
            elements of the Gothic novel. Deals with Radcliffe's "stage
            setting skill," the difference between settings (which are me-
            dieval) and plots (which are clearly seventeenth and eigh-
            teenth century). Compared to Walpole and Reeve, only
            Radcliffe has a clear sense of the romantic. Traces Radcliffe's
            use of landscape back to Milton, Spenser, and MacPherson.
            Discusses her handling of the supernatural and of suspense,
            her heroes and heroines, and her characters' sentimentality.

T38   Sadleir, Michael. *The Northanger Novel: A Footnote to Jane Austen.*
            English Association Pamphlet No. 68. Oxford UP, 1927.

            Examination of *Northanger Abbey*'s "horrid" novels briefly con-
            trasts Radcliffe's and Lewis's sense of the Gothic.

1928

T39   Foster, James R. "Charlotte Smith, Pre-Romantic Novelist."
            PMLA 43 (1928): 163-75.

            Discussion of Smith includes consideration of her influence
            on Radcliffe.

T40   Sadleir, Michael. "Poems by Ann Radcliffe." *TLS* 29 (1928):
            242.

            Letter to *TLS* finds that the Preface to the 1816 edition of

The Poems of Mrs. Ann Radcliffe suggests (mistakenly) that Radcliffe was dead or "no longer 'on the map'" as an important writer. Wonders whether Radcliffe may have been physically and mentally ill at the time the volume was published: "Is it possible that Ann Radcliffe really *was* mentally afflicted; at one time seemed so ill that her death might momentarily be expected, or, at any rate, that no hope of recovery was entertained?" Speculates that these were the circumstances surrounding the publication of this volume, which would have been withdrawn when Radcliffe unexpectedly recovered.

T41   Thorp, Willard. "The Stage Adventures of Some Gothic Novels." *PMLA* 43 (1928): 476-86.

Discusses adaptions of Radcliffe's novels.

1929

T42   Horner, Joyce M. *The English Women Novelists and their Connection with the Feminist Movement (1688-1797).* [*Smith College Studies in Modern Languages* 11 (1929-30).] Northampton, MA: Smith College, 1929-30. 68-78.

Slightly revised M.A. thesis deals with Radcliffe's profits, compares Radcliffe to Walpole and Reeve, criticizes Radcliffe's explained supernatural, praises her scenery.

T43   Messac, Régis. "*Les Mystères du Château d'Udolphe.*" *Le Detective Novel et l'influence de la pensée scientifique.* Paris: Edouard Champion, 1929. 158-177.

Relates the persecuted maiden theme to later detective fiction.

T44   Tompkins, J.M.S. "Ramond de Carbonnières, Grosley, and Mrs. Radcliffe." *Review of English Studies* 5 (1929): 294-301.

P.J. Grosley's *New Observations on Italy and its Inhabitants* was a source for *Udolpho* and *The Italian*; Ramond de Carbonnières' *Observations faites dans les Pyreneés* probably influenced *Udolpho*.

T45   Woolf, Virginia. "Phases of Fiction." 1929. *Granite and Rainbow.* London: Hogarth Press, 1958. 93-145.

Briefly compares Radcliffe to Scott and Stevenson. Characterizes *Udolpho* as "a good test of the romantic attitude, since Mrs. Radcliffe pushes the liberties of romance to the extreme" (108). Applauds Radcliffe's descriptions of scenery and her emotional intensity, but in Radcliffe, "the absurdity is evident, the wheels of the machine are visible and the grinding is heard" (109).

1930

T46   Burra, Peter. "Baroque and Gothic Sentimentalism." *Farrago.* Ed. Peter Burra. Oxford: Simon Nowell Smith, 1930. 1: 159-82.

Praises Radcliffe's Coleridgean and Wordsworthian elements.

T47   Farrand, Margaret. "*Udolpho* and *Childe Harold.*" *Modern Language Notes* 45 (1930): 220-21.

Childe Harold echoes description of Venice in *Udolpho.*

1931

T48   Freeman, R. Austin. Introduction. *The Mysteries of Udolpho.* 1931. London: Dent (Everyman's Library), 1973. v-xi.

Praises Radcliffe's scenery. Finds explanations of the supernatural "satisfying and conclusive" (ix), but criticizes the withholding of information about Emily's observations since the reader sees through Emily's eyes. Notes, but is untroubled by, historical inaccuracies and anachronisms.

T49   Kooiman-Van Middendorp, Gerarda Maria. "Ann Radcliffe (1764-1823)." *The Hero in the Feminine Novel.* 1931. NY: Haskell House, 1966.

Considers the character of Valancourt, who "shows traces of the prototype in Richardson. . . . His character is spoilt by the introduction of Fielding's motives" (37-38). Finds no character development in Radcliffe.

T50   Steeves, Harrison. Introduction. *Three Eighteenth-Century Romances.* 1931. NY: Scribner's, 1971.

Introduction to *Romance of the Forest* [abridged version], *Otranto,* and *Vathek* criticizes Radcliffe's plots and style. Although praises Radcliffe's "imaginative vigor and romantic beauty," condemns her as redundant and inconsistent. Characterizes Radcliffe's politics as "insular" and "childish."

1932

T51   Leavis, Q.D. *Fiction and the Reading Public.* 1932. London: Chatto and Windus, 1965.

Calls Scott "another Mrs. Radcliffe" (139). Praises *Udolpho* for the very anachronisms that most critics consider defects:

> The superb absence of any historical sense is the saving of *The Mysteries of Udolpho.* It proves conclusively that late eighteenth-century taste was still sure of itself, that there was a culture strong enough to absorb everything alien. Mrs. Radcliffe has no perceptible misgivings in treating a story of the year 1568 as the history of a contemporary young lady of delicate sensibility . . . . (140)

T52   McKillop, Alan D. "Mrs. Radcliffe on the Supernatural in Poetry." *Journal of English and Germanic Philology* 31 (1932): 352-59.

Discussion of Radcliffe's posthumously published essay, "On the Supernatural in Poetry." Gothic writers "sought to shelter themselves under Shakespeare's authority" (353).

T53   Sharp, R. Farquharson. *The Reader's Guide to Everyman's Library.* NY: E.P. Dutton & Co., 1932.

Lists R.A. Freeman's edition of *Udolpho.*

T54   Tompkins, J.M.S. *The Popular Novel in England 1770-1800.* 1932. Lincoln: U of Nebraska P, 1961.

Discusses the two veins of Gothic Romance, the first epitomized by the works of Radcliffe, the second, later stage, by the works of Lewis. Analyzes Radcliffe's development of plot and of psychological motivation. Radcliffe's explanations of the supernatural constitute "the vice of her method." Discusses Radcliffe's sources.

1933

T55   Praz, Mario. *The Romantic Agony.* Trans. Angus Davidson. 1933. London: Oxford UP, 1954.

Very few examples from Radcliffe's work appear. Points out her influence on other writers such as Byron and Italian novelists A. Manzoni and F.D. Guerrazzi. In sexist terms,

notes Radcliffe's use of the persecuted maiden motif: "Like
Mrs. Radcliffe, other authoresses also adopted the persecuted
woman as a character; but there may be nothing more in this
than another of the many manifestations of feminine imita-
tiveness. As the literary tradition has been the monopoly of
man, at any rate up till the present, it is natural that women
writers should slavishly adopt in their works the masculine
point of view" (113).

1934

T56   Baker, Ernest A. *The History of the English Novel.* 10 vols. London: H.F. & G. Witherby, 1924-39. [Vol. 5 published in 1934.]
5: 192-205.

Considers Radcliffe's works as the best of the Gothic genre.
Radcliffe's greatest contribution was her picturesque paintings of atmosphere, influenced by Nicolas Poussin, Claude
Lorrain, Salvator Rosa, and Guido Reni. Points to Radcliffe's
lack of realism: "Banditti are always lurking in the woods; she
seems to regard them as a kind of local fauna" (5:195). Finds
all her heroines full of sensibility, evidenced by their enthusiasm for nature. This sensibility extends to her heroes, since
"her heroes are all heroines . . ." (5: 204). Discusses Radcliffe's
development through the course of her novels: *The Castles of
Athlin and Dunbayne* is "negligible" (5:193). Although *A Sicilian Romance* is the first real novel of suspense, it is "crowded
with incident" (5: 193). *Romance of the Forest* furthers the
genre of the suspense novel. Discusses landscapes and interi-
ors in *Udolpho,* suspense in *The Italian,* and "the unfortunate
ghost" and "tedious" historical references in *Gaston de
Blondeville,* her "dullest" novel (5: 203). Briefly touches on
the explained supernatural and on Radcliffe's influence and
imitators.

T57   Marshall, Roderick. *Italy in English Literature 1755-1815.* NY:
Columbia UP, 1934.

Attributing spiritual powers to the Italian landscape, Radcliffe
inspired the Romantics. Her novels that are set in Italy (*A
Sicilian Romance, Udolpho,* and *The Italian*) describe landscape
she had never visited. Her descriptions were, instead, influenced by paintings and by travel literature. The heroines of her
Italian novels progress in their understanding of nature from

Julia (*A Sicilian Romance*), who rarely seeks comfort in nature, to Emily (*Udolpho*), who regards nature more frequently and more reverentially, to Ellena (*The Italian*), who turns to nature for spiritual communion. Considers Radcliffe's imitators, concluding that "In the hands of the terror novelists Italian character was simply torn to shreds, and it often seems as if their vogue must surely have damaged, if not actually overthrown, the good work of the sentimental travellers" (251).

T58 Mehrotra, K.K. *Horace Walpole and the English Novel*. NY: Russell and Russell, 1934.

Although it is impossible to prove that Radcliffe read *Otranto*, she seems to have been influenced by Walpole's work.

T59 Roberts, R. Ellis. "The Other Side." *Life and Letters* 10 (1934): 691-701.

Brief discussion of Radcliffe links her works to MacPherson's *Ossian*.

T60 Rogers, Winfield H. "The Reaction Against Melodramatic Sentimentality in the English Novel, 1796-1830." *PMLA* 49 (1934): 98-122.

Briefly considers Austen's use of *Udolpho* in *Northanger Abbey*. Mentions parody of Radcliffe in Barrett's *The Heroine*.

1935

T61 Monk, Samuel H. *The Sublime: A Study of Critical Theories in XVIII-Century England*. NY: MLA, 1935.

Brief consideration of Radcliffe finds her novels almost totally composed of sublime elements. The greatest "landscape novelist of all time" (217), Radcliffe's novels constitute "expressions of Burkean sublimity" (219).

1936

T62 Hillhouse, James T. *The Waverley Novels and their Critics*. Minneapolis: U of Minnesota P, 1936.

Scattered references to Radcliffe.

T63 Streeter, Harold Wade. *The Eighteenth Century English Novel in French Translation*. 1936. NY: Benjamin Blom Inc., 1970.

Translation of the novels of Radcliffe and of Lewis initiated the French vogue for the Gothic.

T64 Summers, Montague. "The Illustrations of the 'Gothick' Novels." *Connoisseur* 98 (1936): 266-71.

Briefly touches on Radcliffe's descriptions of ruins. Includes several illustrations of early editions of *The Italian*.

T65 Utter, Robert Palfrey and Gwendolyn Bridges Needham. *Pamela's Daughters*. NY: Macmillan, 1936.

Mockingly observes that Radcliffe "exhibits the sentimental heroine at full length" (129). Pays Radcliffe a back-handed compliment: "Her heroines seem genuinely vertebrate in comparison with some of the moist unpleasant jellyfish spawned by her contemporaries and predecessors" (130). Although her heroines have delicate airs, the terrors they are subjected to necessitate their fortitude since "not even Mrs. Radcliffe could terrorize a jellyfish; there must be a spine for the chills to run up and down" (130). Radcliffe's heroines inherited from Pamela their habit of fainting.

1937

T66 Whitt, Celia. "Poe and *The Mysteries of Udolpho*." *University of Texas Studies in English* 17 (1937): 124-31.

Poe derived details, situations, and characters for his short story "The Assignation" from *Udolpho*. Poe's Mentoni resembles Radcliffe's Montoni in more than name.

T67 Wright, Walter Francis. "Sensibility in English Prose Fiction 1760-1814: A Reinterpretation." *Illinois Studies in Language and Literature* 22 (1937): 9-154.

Discusses Radcliffe's landscape descriptions, her "ultra-sentimental" plots and characterization, her influences, and her reputation. Despite Radcliffe's genius, her role in literary history has been minor: "Today, students of English prose fiction concede some historical importance to her; yet they read with amusement chapters which the novelist herself wrote with serious intent." The reason for the ridicule is that " . . . Mrs. Radcliffe possessed, in almost equal degree, the qualities of a great writer and those of a mediocre one. Her works show the beauty which sensibility combined with imagination can discover and create, but they show, too, the excesses which lead to decay" (79). Goes on to consider *The Children of the Abbey* (1796), Regina Roche's Radcliffean imitation.

1938

T68 Summers, Montague. *The Gothic Quest: A History of the Gothic Novel.* NY: Russell and Russell, 1938.

Radcliffe's work includes both the terrible and the sentimental. Ossian influenced Radcliffe, who, in turn, influenced the French novelists. Criticizes Radcliffe's explanations of mystery. Discusses Lewis's praise of Radcliffe and compares Radcliffe ("the romanticist of the Gothic novel") and Lewis ("the realist"). Radcliffe uses ruins not to symbolize the end of feudalism, but rather to heighten emotion.

T69 Reviewed in *TLS*, Dec. 24, 1938, pp. 815 and 817.

T70 Tuttle, Donald Reuel. "*Christabel* Sources in Percy's *Reliques* and the Gothic Romance." *PMLA* 53 (1938): 445-75.

Includes discussion of Coleridge's indebtedness to Radcliffe.

1939

T71 Blakey, Dorothy. *The Minerva Press 1790-1820.* London: Printed for the Bibliographical Society at the University Press, Oxford, 1939 (for 1935).

Although *The Fate of Velina de Guidova* and *Radzivil* have been attributed to Ann Radcliffe, they are probably by Mary Ann Radcliffe.

T72 Block, Andrew. *The English Novel 1740-1850.* 1939. London: Dawsons, 1967.

Radcliffe entry consists of transcriptions of title pages of earliest editions of her works.

1941

T73 Mayo, Robert D. "Ann Radcliffe and Ducray-Duminil." *Modern Language Review* 36 (1941): 501-505.

Argues that Ducray-Duminil's *Alexis* influenced *Romance of the Forest.*

1943

T74   Mayo, Robert D. "How Long was Gothic Fiction in Vogue?"
           Modern Language Notes 58 (1943):58-64.

           Analyzes *Lady's Magazine* to find that Gothics began to be
           popular the year of Radcliffe's first smash hit (1791) and
           continued to be popular after Radcliffe's last novel.

T75   Wagenknecht, Edward. *Cavalcade of the English Novel.* NY: Holt,
           Rinehart and Winston, 1943.

           Objects to Radcliffe's anachronisms, attitude towards the su-
           pernatural, and characterization but praises her landscapes.
           Discusses the sensibility of Radcliffe's heroines, whose
           "[p]rudery actually inspires grandeur" (120). Considers *The
           Italian* Radcliffe's "masterpiece."

1945

T76   Sypher, Wylie. "Social Ambiguity in a Gothic Novel." *Parti-
           san Review* 12 (1945): 50-60.

           Discerns a subtext of socio-economic paradox and of ambi-
           guity in moral and aesthetic values in *Udolpho.*

1946

T77   McCullough, Bruce. "The Gothic Romance." *Representative
           English Novelists: Defoe to Conrad.* NY: Harper and Brothers,
           1946. 84-96.

           Perfunctory discussion of Radcliffe concentrates on *Udolpho,*
           briefly comparing Emily to Richardson's Clarissa and to
           Fielding's Sophia.

1947

T78   Bowen, Elizabeth. Introduction. *Uncle Silas.* By Joesph
           Sheridan Le Fanu. London: The Cresset Press, 1947. 7-23.

           Briefly suggests that Le Fanu was influenced by Radcliffe.

1948

T79   Baugh, Albert. *A Literary History of England.* NY: Appleton-
           Century-Crofts, 1948.

Brief examination of Radcliffe's novels patronizingly finds that "a quiet lady who never had an adventure in her life, is the arch-Gothicizer of them all" (1194).

T80 MacCarthy, Bridget G. *The Later Women Novelists 1744-1818* [also known as *The Female Pen*]. NY: William Salloch, 1948.

Considers Radcliffe's development: *Athlin and Dunbayne* and *Sicilian Romance* are "first totterings" (164); *The Romance of the Forest* is an advance, which first displays the power of her poetic descriptions. *Udolpho*'s "perfections are far greater than its faults" (173). Considers *The Italian* Radcliffe's best performance. In *Gaston* finds the ghost to be a "flat-footed apparition" that "alarms far less than the tiniest mouse scurrying in the wainscot of Udolpho" (183). In general criticizes Radcliffe for her stock characters, her negative attitude towards Catholicism, and her interpolated poems, which are "worthless in themselves and absurd in their settings" (168). Like Kavanagh, laments Radcliffe's lack of education.

1949

T81 Foster, James R. *History of the Pre-Romantic Novel in England.* NY: MLA; London: Oxford UP, 1949.

Describes Radcliffe as the "end of a phase" (261). Her strongest talent was her imagination: "She was the inventor of melodrama in technicolor, the great impresario of beauty, wonder and terror" (262). If Radcliffe's first two novels are mediocre, she comes of age with *The Romance of the Forest.* Considers *The Italian* her best effort.

T82 Ruff, William. "Ann Radcliffe, or, The Hand of Taste." *The Age of Johnson: Essays Presented to Chauncey Brewster Tinker.* Ed. Frederick Hilles. New Haven: Yale UP, 1949.

A casual, fairly negative consideration of Radcliffe as a writer of "the novel of taste" (186).

6

TWENTIETH-CENTURY CRITICISM, PART II: 1950–PRESENT (TC)

1951

TC1   Havens, Raymond D. "Ann Radcliffe's Nature Descriptions." *Modern Language Notes* 66 (1951): 251-55.

Observes the difference between Radcliffe's genuine sensitivity to nature and the overly dramatized descriptions in her novels. Recognizes the nature scenes in the novels as literary device.

TC2   Patterson, Charles I. "The Authenticity of Coleridge's Reviews of Gothic Romances." *JEGP* 50 (1951): 517-21.

Argues against attribution of *Udolpho* review in *Critical Review* to Coleridge. See Erdman (1959) and Roper (1972).

1952

TC3   Kunitz, Stanley and Howard Haycraft, eds. "Radcliffe, Mrs. Ann (Ward)." *British Authors before 1800: A Biographical Dictionary.* NY: H.W. Wilson Company, 1952. 426-27.

Although grudgingly acknowledges that Radcliffe was a seminal figure in the development of English literature, finds that she is "practically unreadable today" (427). Even in her three best works, *The Romance of the Forest, The Mysteries of Udolpho*, and *The Italian*, "there is the same dreary succession of trials of a persecuted heroine, conventionally represented, of dangers and terrors that peter out to nothing, and of final victory over the lady's enemies . . ." (427).

TC4   Neill, S. Diana. *A Short History of the English Novel.* NY:
Macmillan, 1952.

Includes brief survey of Radcliffe's works.

1954

TC5   Allen, Walter. *The English Novel.* NY: E.P. Dutton, 1954.

Although devotes more space to Radcliffe than does Ian Watt,
who barely mentions her in his seminal *Rise of the Novel,*
Allen's consideration of Radcliffe is fairly brief. Discusses
Radcliffe's use of landscape in relation to Emily, who is "a
dim enough character, but . . . she is incarnate sensibility,
and her function in the novel is simply to feel, to feel the
appropriate emotions of wonder, awe, and terror" (101).
Radcliffe uses her novel to elicit similar emotions from the
reader. Compared to Radliffe's use of environment, which
overwhelms characters, "Richardson, Fielding, Smollett, [and]
Miss Burney play out their actions on bare boards" (101).

1956

TC6   *The Confessional of the Black Penitents.* With wood-engravings
by Philip Ross. London: Folio Society, 1956.

Edition of *The Italian* with unsigned brief introduction.

1957

TC7   Moorman, Mary. *William Wordsworth: A Biography.* Oxford:
The Clarendon Press, 1957.

Briefly notes influence of *Romance of the Forest* on Wordsworth
(307-308).

TC8   Varma, Devendra P. "Mrs. Ann Radcliffe: The Craft of Terror." *The Gothic Flame.* 1957. NY: Russell & Russell, 1966. 85-
128.

Influential and pioneering examination of Radcliffe by the
person who has, perhaps, done the most to insure her place
in the canon. Traces her style through the novels and discusses her use of the "explained supernatural." Outlines her
contributions to the development of the psychological novel
in terms of the structure of the novel, the spotlighting of
individual scenes, the refinement of suspense, the use of

romantic scenery, the characterization of villain-heroes, and the use of dialogue to reveal character and to advance action. Concludes that in Radcliffe we find "the finest flowering of the novels of Terror" (128).

1958

TC9   Preu, James. "The Tale of Terror." *English Journal* 47 (1958): 243-47.

This general discussion of the Gothic briefly touches on Radcliffe's explained supernatural and her descriptions. Backhanded praise finds that "Of the many women who tried their hands at the Gothic novel, Mrs. Radcliffe was one of the most successful" (245).

1959

TC10   Erdman, David. "Immoral Acts of a Library Cormorant: The Extent of Coleridge's Contributions to the *Critical Review.*" *Bulletin of the New York Public Library* 63 (Sept.-Nov. 1959): 433-454, 515-530, 575-587.

Argues that Coleridge did, in fact, write the reviews of *Udolpho* and *The Italian* in *Critical Review.* See Patterson (1951) and Roper (1972) for the dispute about authorship.

TC11   Humphrey, George. "'Victor ou l'enfant de la forêt' et le roman terrifiant." *French Review* 33 (1959): 137-46.

Discusses English influence, especially Radcliffe's.

1960

TC12   Eenhoorn, Michael, ed. *The Mysteries of Udolpho.* Vol. 7 of *The Classics of Mystery.* NY: Juniper Press, [1960].

Abridged version with one-page introduction.

TC13   Fiedler, Leslie. *Love and Death in the American Novel.* NY: Criterion Books, 1960.

Brief discussion of Radcliffe's influence considers the middle of her novels "in their compulsive repetitiveness a self-duplicating nightmare from which it is impossible to wake" (107). Compares *The Italian* to *Clarissa.*

TC14 Stevenson, Lionel. *The English Novel: A Panorama.* 1960. Westport, Connecticut: Greenwood Press, 1978.

Her use of the unconscious accounts for Radcliffe's popularity: "In departing from realism Mrs. Radcliffe stumbled upon the whole realm of the unconscious" (165).

TC15 Ware, Malcolm. "Mrs. Radcliffe's 'Picturesque Embellishment'" *Tennessee Studies in Literature* 5 (1960): 67-71.

Argues that picturesque description keeps Radcliffe's novels from passing from terror to horror.

1961

TC16 Bland, D. S. "Endangering the Reader's Neck: Background Description in the Novel." *Criticism* (1961) 3: 121-39.

Discusses the use of landscape by the early novelists, including Radcliffe. Considers the influence of landscape painting.

TC17 Bradbrook, Frank W. "Sources of Jane Austen's Ideas about Nature in *Mansfield Park.*" *Notes and Queries* (1961): 222-24.

Notes parallels between *Udolpho* and *Mansfield Park.*

1962

TC18 Coolidge, Archibald C., Jr. "Charles Dickens and Mrs. Radcliffe: A Farewell to Wilkie Collins." *Dickensian* 58 (1962): 112-116.

Discusses Radcliffe's techniques of arousing anxiety and curiosity and their influence on the Gothic nature of Dickens' works.

TC19 Mayo, Robert D. *The English Novel in the Magazines 1740-1815.* Evanston: Northwestern UP, 1962.

Includes scattered references to the representation of Radcliffe in contemporary magazines.

TC20 Nelson, Lowry, Jr. "Night Thoughts on the Gothic Novel." *Yale Review* 52 (1962): 235-57.

Finds early attempts of the Gothic novel at psychological complexity and depth disappointing. Brief derogatory mention of Radcliffe's novels, which "now seem more like childish fantasies than evocations of primal horror" (238).

TC21   Thorslev, Peter, Jr. *The Byronic Hero: Types and Prototypes.* Minneapolis: Minnesota UP, 1962.

Considers Montoni and Schedoni as precursor of the Byronic hero.

1963

TC22   Beaty, Frederick L. "Mrs. Radcliffe's Fading Gleam." *Philological Quarterly* 42 (1963): 126-29.

The "nature myth" in *Udolpho* influenced both Coleridge and Wordsworth.

TC23   Renwick, W.L. *English Literature 1789-1815.* Oxford: Clarendon Press, 1963.

Emphasizes Radcliffe's imagination and her use of picturesque description, discussing the novels in terms of *The Journey.*

TC24   Ware, Malcolm. *Sublimity in the Novels of Ann Radcliffe: A Study of the Influence upon her Craft of Edmund Burke's "Enquiry into the Origin of our Ideas of the Sublime and Beautiful."* Copenhagen: Ejnar Munksgaard, 1963.

Short study (62 pp.) discusses Burke's influence on Radcliffe. Considers as integral to the terror of her descriptions Burke's seven sources of sublimity (obscurity, power, privation, vastness, infinity, difficulty, and magnificence).

TC25   Wright, Andrew. Introduction. *The Castle of Otranto, The Mysteries of Udolpho* [abridged], *Northanger Abbey.* NY: Holt, Rinehart and Winston, 1963. vii-xxi.

Brief remarks on Radcliffe praise her novels for their use of the unconscious, despite their "crudity of construction" (xiv).

1964

TC26   Bernard, Kenneth. "Charles Brockden Brown and the Sublime." *The Personalist* 45 (1964): 235-49.

Influence of Radcliffe, Burke, and Gilpin on Brown's nature descriptions. Radcliffe's scenery is decorative, whereas Brown's is functional.

TC27   Decottignies, Jean. "A l'Occasion du deuxième centenaire de la naissance d'Anne Radcliffe: Un Domaine 'maudit' dans les lettres françaises aux environs de 1800." *Revue des Sciences Humaines* 116 (1964): 447-475.

The anniversary of Radcliffe's birth provides the occasion for this study of the popularity of Radcliffe's novels in France from around 1797-1810.

TC28   Lévy, Maurice. "Une nouvelle source d'Anne Radcliffe: *Les Mémoires du Comte de Comminge.*" *Caliban* 1 (1964): 149-56.

Argues that these memoirs inspired *Sicilian Romance*.

TC29   Schneider, Marcel. *La Littérature fantastique en France.* Paris: Fayard, 1964.

Recognizes Radcliffe's influence on the fantastic in French Romanticism.

TC30   Thomas, Donald. "The First Poetess of Romantic Fiction: Ann Radcliffe, 1764-1823." *English* 15 (1964): 91-95.

Radcliffe is not only a Gothic novelist, but also—based on subject matter—a typical writer of romantic fiction. Discusses Radcliffe's use of anticipated terror and her settings.

TC31   Trainer, James. *Ludwig Tieck: From Gothic to Romantic.* London, The Hague, Paris: Mouton, 1964.

Deals with the influence of Gothic novelists, especially Radcliffe, on Tieck.

TC32   Rev. in *TLS*, Sept. 17, 1964, p. 860.

1965

TC33   Lévy, Maurice. "Shakespeare et le roman 'gothique.'" *Caliban* ns 1 (1965): 47-63.

Notes similarities between Shakespeare's plays and the novels of Walpole, Reeve, Radcliffe, and Lewis.

TC34   Steeves, Harrison R. *Before Jane Austen: The Shaping of the English Novel in the Eighteenth Century.* NY, Chicago, San Francisco: Holt, Rinehart and Winston, 1965.

Describes Radcliffe as the "unequalled begetter" of the Gothics, who "helped in the restoration of life to the romantic tradition." Her last three novels show her maturity and mastery of the medium; her villains "command attention." Although she was a bad poet, her fiction is enhanced by her poetic tendencies. In *Udolpho*, Radcliffe "earns the very highest marks for sensibility." Makes some attempt to account for her popularity: "The answer. . . is not that the taste of her day was deplorable. It was, but it can still be debated whether that bad taste explains her romances or the romances explain the bad taste."

1966

TC35 Allen, M. L. "The Black Veil: Three Versions of a Symbol." *English Studies* 47 (1966): 286-89.

Discusses the black veil in *Udolpho* and in short stories by Dickens ("The Black Veil") and Hawthorne ("The Minister's Black Veil").

TC36 Dobrée, Bonamy. Introduction. *The Mysteries of Udolpho*. London: Oxford UP, 1966. vii-xvi.

A biographical and critical introduction that takes up matters such as Radcliffe's characters, structure, and influence. Distinguishing between "terror" and "horror," argues that *Udolpho* is a "horror novel" and a "novel of sentiment." Text is the definitive edition with explanatory notes by Frederick Garber.

TC37 Rev. "Extricating Emily." *Time* 22 April 1966: 88.

This review of the Oxford *Udolpho* acknowledges Radcliffe's influence even as it mocks her novel: ". . . if in 1794 her virginal vaporings came on as symptoms of high sensibility, in 1966, they come off as conventions of high comedy. All unintentionally, *Udolpho* is one of the funniest books ever written. . . ." Illustrated with a reproduction of the Bettman Archives' portrait of Radcliffe.

TC38 Graham, John. "Character Description and Meaning in the Romantic Novel." *Studies in Romanticism* 5 (1966): 208-18.

Briefly discusses Radcliffe's use of physiognomy.

TC39 Macherey, Pierre. *Pour une théorie de la production littéraire*. Paris: Maspéro, 1966.

Includes several brief references to Radcliffe.

1967

TC40   Arnaud, Pierre. "Un Document inédit: le Contrat des *Mysteries of Udolpho.*" *Etudes Anglaises* 20 (1967): 55-57.

Discusses (and reproduces) the contract for *Udolpho* (now in the Sadleir-Black Collection in the U of Virginia Library). According to the terms of the contract, Radcliffe was to receive 500 pounds.

1968

TC41   Emden, Cecil S. "The Composition of *Northanger Abbey.*" *Review of English Studies* ns 19 (1968): 279-287.

Argues that Austen wrote the main, non-Gothic portions of the novel around 1794 and added the burlesque of *Udolpho* and other Gothic novels around 1798.

TC42   Frye, Northrop. *A Study of English Romanticism.* NY: Random House, 1968.

Mentions Radcliffe in passing while discussing the sublime oracular sense of nature:

> Mrs. Radcliffe, it is true, writes from a relentlessly enlightened point of view that first summons up a supernatural mystery and then sandbags it with a rational explanation, but she shows her adherence to the oracular tradition in her sensitive heroines, who follow the general Gothic pattern. We may wonder why any literary convention should have produced these absurd creatures, drizzling like a Scotch mist and fainting at every crisis in the plot; but there is clearly something mediumistic about such females . . . . (29)

TC43   Garber, Frederick. Introduction. *The Italian.* 1968. London: Oxford UP, 1989. vii-xv.

Discusses lack of realism, characterization of Schedoni, and use of the Inquisition. Considers the novel in terms of various genres (*Bildungsroman,* novel of sentiment, fairy tale).

TC44   Rev. in *TLS* No. 3,454 (1968): 472.

TC45   Hart, Francis Russell. "The Experience of Character in the English Gothic Novel." *Experience in the Novel: Selected Papers* *from the English Institute.* Ed. Roy Harvey Pearce. NY and London: Columbia UP, 1968. 83-105.

Wide-ranging discussion of character in works including *Udolpho, The Monk, Caleb Williams, Wuthering Heights, Jane Eyre, Frankenstein,* and *Melmoth the Wanderer.* Discussion of *Udolpho* distinguishes between character and role.

TC46 Lévy, Maurice. *Le Roman "gothique" anglais, 1764-1824.* Toulouse: Association des publications de la Faculté des lettres et sciences humaines de Toulouse, 1968.

Massive scholarly study of the English Gothic. Compares Radcliffe to Walpole and to Lewis. Discusses Radcliffe's descriptions and use of suspense. Includes discussion of gothic parodies. Ninety pages of bibliographies and indices.

TC47 Rev. by Robert Hume in *Poe Studies* 4 (1971): 58-59.

TC48 Praz, Mario. Introduction. *Three Gothic Novels* [*Otranto; Vathek; Frankenstein*]. 1968. NY: Penguin, 1986. 7-35.

Lumps Radcliffe together with Lewis and Sade as belonging "to the same mental climate, the climate which produced so many incarnations of the theme of the persecuted maiden . . ." (14-15).

TC49 Varma, Devendra P. Introduction. *The Italian.* 2 vols. NY: Russell and Russell, 1968. i-xxv.

Discusses sources, use of the picturesque, influence, and publication history.

TC50 Williams, Ioan, ed. *Sir Walter Scott on Novelists and Fiction.* NY: Barnes and Noble, 1968.

Reworking and collating texts from Scott's *Lives of the Novelists,* judges Radcliffe's main characteristic to be the explained supernatural.

1969

TC51 Heller, Lynne Epstein. "Mrs. Radcliffe's Landscapes: The Influence of Three Landscape Painters on her Nature Descriptions." *Hartford Studies in Literature* 1 (1969): 107-20.

Identifies the influence of Claude Lorrain, Salvator Rosa, and Nicholas Poussin on Radcliffe's work. Radcliffe painted "in words the landscapes [they] had wrought in their art." Includes plates.

TC52   Hume, Robert D. "Gothic Versus Romantic: A Revaluation of the Gothic Novel." *PMLA* 84 (1969): 282-90.

Distinguishes between Radcliffe's novel of terror and Lewis' novel of horror. Traces the development of the latter in the nineteenth and twentieth centuries.

TC53   For debate between Robert Hume and Robert Platzner inspired by this article, see " 'Gothic versus Romantic': A Rejoinder." *PMLA* 86 (1971): 266-74.

TC54   Korninger, Siegfried. "Radcliffe: *The Mysteries of Udolpho.*" *Der englische Roman.* Düsseldorf, Germany: Bagel, 1969. 1: 312-337.

Discusses Radcliffe's descriptions of nature and her contributions to the psychological novel.

TC55   Miyoshi, Masao. *The Divided Self: A Perspective on the Literature of the Victorians.* NY: New York UP, 1969.

Includes brief discussion of Radcliffe.

TC56   Quennell, Peter. "The Moon Stood Still on Strawberry Hill." *Horizon Magazine* 11 (1969): 113-19.

Includes brief discussion of *Udolpho.*

TC57   Swigart, Ford H., Jr. "Ann Radcliffe's Veil Imagery." *Studies in the Humanities* 1 (1969): 55-59.

A study of Radcliffe's veil imagery, including actual veils, facial expressions, clouds, etc.

1970

TC58   Johnson, Edgar. *Sir Walter Scott: The Great Unknown.* 2 vols. NY: Macmillan, 1970.

Brief references to Radcliffe's influence on Scott and to her inclusion in Ballantyne's *Novelists' Library.*

TC59   Poenicke, Klaus. "'Schönheit im Schosse des Schreckens': Raumgefüge und Menschenbild im englischen Schauer-roman." *Archiv für das Studium der neueren Sprachen und Literaturen* 207 (1970): 1-19.

An analysis of Walpole, Reeve, Lewis, and Radcliffe. Discusses Radcliffe's characters in terms of spacial relationships.

TC60 Radcliffe, Ann. *The Castles of Athlin and Dunbayne.* Belles Lettres in English. Ed. Robert Donald Spector and Martin Tucker. NY: Johnson Reprint, 1970.

Facsimile edition with no introduction.

TC61 _____. *Romance of the Forest.* 3 vols. Belles Lettres in English. Ed. Robert Donald Spector and Martin Tucker. NY: Johnson Reprint, 1970.

Facsimile edition with no introduction.

TC62 Todorov, Tzvetan. *The Fantastic: A Structural Approach to a Literary Genre.* Trans. Richard Howard. 1970. Cleveland: The Press of Case Western Reserve U, 1973.

Refers to Radcliffe in consideration of the fantastic, which is located between the marvelous (where the supernatural is accepted, as in Walpole, Lewis, and Maturin) and the uncanny (where the supernatural is explained, as in Reeve and Radcliffe). The fantastic "lasts only as long as a certain hesitation: a hesitation common to reader and character, who must decide whether or not what they perceive derives from 'reality' as it exists in the common opinion. At the story's end, the reader . . . opts for one solution or the other [the marvelous or the uncanny], and thereby emerges from the fantastic." (40). Radcliffe produces the effect of the fantastic, but only up to the point where the reader suspects a rational explanation. Conversely, it resides in Lewis, but only up to the point where the reader suspects no rational explanation will be possible.

TC63 Wright, Eugene P. "A Divine Analysis of *The Romance of the Forest.*" *Discourse* 13 (1970): 379-87.

Analyzes reaction of Joanna Southcott (the nineteenth-century religious mystic) to *Romance of the Forest.*

1971

TC64 Blondel, Jacques. "On 'Metaphysical Prisons.'" *Durham University Journal* 32 (1971): 133-38.

Touches on Radcliffe, whose prisons contrast with the sublime. Radcliffe's final vision is of daylight rather than darkness.

TC65   Breitinger, Eckard. *Der Tod im englischen Roman um 1800.* Göppingen: Alfred Kummerle, 1971. (Tübinger Dissertation).

Study of death in the English novel examines works of Godwin and both Shelleys. Includes references to Radcliffe.

TC66   Christensen, Merton A. "*Udolpho, Horrid Mysteries*, and Coleridge's Machinery of the Imagination." *Wordsworth Circle* 2 (1971): 153-159.

Considers *Udolpho* and Carl Grosse's *Horrid Mysteries* in terms of Coleridge's theory of art and his use of the Gothic in *Ancient Mariner.*

TC67   Kroeber, Karl. *Styles in Fictional Structure.* Princeton: Princeton UP, 1971.

Brief reflection on Gothic romances suggests that most Gothic novelists, such as Walpole, Lewis, and Mary Shelley, explain little. If Radcliffe explains her supernatural effects, she fails to explain other features of her novels such as the violent personalities, unusual architecture, awesome scenery, and extreme emotions. Points to a motif in Radcliffe that is unprecedented in literature: "*transport,* travel combined with rapture" (116).

TC68   Radcliffe, Ann. *Sicilian Romance.* 2 vols. Belles Lettres in English. Ed. Robert Donald Spector and Martin Tucker. NY: Johnson Reprint, 1971.

Facsimile with no introduction.

1972

TC69   Adams, Donald K. "The Second Mrs. Radcliffe." *Mystery and Detection Annual.* [Ed. Donald Adams?] Beverly Hills: Donald Adams, 1972. 48-64.

After briefly discussing the many imitators of Ann Ward Radcliffe, considers Mary Ann Radcliffe in some detail.

TC70   Gose, Elliott, Jr. *Imagination Indulged: The Irrational in the Nineteenth-Century Novel.* Montreal and London: McGill-Queen's UP, 1972.

Chapters on the Gothic novel and on *The Monk* deal in passing with Radcliffe's attempt to "humanize the irrational" (23).

TC71   Jeune, Simon. "Autour de *L'Abbesse de Castro.*" *Travaux de linguistique et de littérature (Université de Strasbourg)* 20 (1972): 99-111.

Argues that Radcliffe may have written *The Abbess of Castro.*

TC72   Jones, Howard Mumford. Foreword. *A Sicilian Romance.* NY: Arno, 1972. i-v.

Brief general remarks on the influence of Radcliffe on Poe, the Romantics, the Victorians, and the detective genre. The only (brief) reference to *A Sicilian Romance* finds its villain "far more entrancing" than Montoni (iv).

TC73   Kiely, Robert. *The Romantic Novel in England.* Cambridge: Harvard UP, 1972.

Features of Radcliffe's prose were so widely imitated that "they were clichés before they had time to become conventions" (65). Consideration of nature finds that Radcliffe's characters are either close enough to nature to "botanize" like St. Aubert, or far enough away to muse. Finds that nature is often impotent. Radcliffe's heroines are usually unable to react or they overreact. Kiely's psychological reading of Emily finds that, far from being the passive "simpering puppets" of critical tradition, Emily and Radcliffe's other hysterical heroines are often "obsessive, implacable, and morbidly excitable women whose moods often make difficult situations worse" (70). *Udolpho* may preach balance and moderation, but Emily's panic is what gives the novel its interest. Although Emily has been compared to Clarissa, Montoni never threatens her sexually. Lacking clear perceptions, Emily, who is ambivalent about Montoni and his associates, is in a state of hysteria in which her fears have power over reality. Radcliffe's contribution is not only introducing Gothic elements into the sentimental novel, but projecting "a nonrational mentality into a total environment" (77).

TC74   Norton, Rictor. "Aesthetic Gothic Horror." *Yearbook of Comparative and General Literature* 21 (1972): 31-40.

Radcliffe's use of the Burkean sublime serves as an example in this exploration of the Gothic's reconciliation of opposites.

TC75   Roper, Derek. "Coleridge, Dyer and *The Mysteries of Udolpho.*" *Notes and Queries* 19 (1972): 287-89.

Claims that Coleridge could not have written a review of *Udolpho* in 1794. See Patterson (1951) and Erdman (1959) for this dispute. Attributes review of *Udolpho* in *Analytical Review* to George Dyer.

TC76   Shroyer, Frederick. Foreword. *The Castles of Athlin and Dunbayne.* NY: Arno, 1972. i-iv.

Briefly discusses Radcliffe's first experiment with the Gothic as possessing intimations of her narrative and descriptive talent.

TC77   Varma, Devendra P. Introduction. *Gaston de Blondeville.* 2 vols. NY: Arno, 1972.

Brief introduction praises Radcliffe's scenery and her villains. Includes the Memoir of Radcliffe that accompanied the original publication.

TC78   Varma, Devendra P. Introduction. *A Sicilian Romance.* NY: Arno, 1972. vii-xxvi.

A general discussion of influence of Burke on Radcliffe. Brief remarks about the novel at hand suggest that here the sublime serves to elevate the mind more than in Radcliffe's first novel and that Radcliffe's writing depends on contrasts such as darkness interrupted by flashes of light.

1973

TC79   Garber, Frederick. "Meaning and Mode in Gothic Fiction." *Studies in Eigtheenth Century Culture* 3 (1973): 155-69.

Explores Gothicism as a confrontation of different modes. In *The Italian* the conventional values of sentimental fiction leave Vivaldi and Ellena unprepared for evil, making for "the comedy of the inappropriate response" (160), when decorum meets malevolence. Radcliffe intellectualizes and humanizes terror, as dangers come from people instead of from supernatural agency.

TC80   Smith, Nelson C. "Sense, Sensibility and Ann Radcliffe." *Studies in English Literature* 13 (1973): 577-90.

Radcliffe did not advocate sensibility. Instead, to criticize sentimental novels, she exposed their heroines to Gothic conventions. Almost twenty years before Austen, Radcliffe articulated the difference between sense and sensibility.

1974

TC81 Brissenden, R. F. *Virtue in Distress: Studies in the Novel of Sentiment from Richardson to Sade.* NY: Harper and Row, 1974.

Briefly discusses the Richardsonian manner in the style of Radcliffe, "an essentially minor and second-rank novelist" (92). The major flaw in Radcliffe's novels is that her virtuous heroines are made to suffer, but their virtue is not the cause of their distress. Instead, their virtue and extreme sensibility simply heighten the horror of their situations.

TC82 Garber, Frederick. Foreword. *The Romance of the Forest.* 3 vols. NY: Arno, 1974. 1: vii-xi.

Foreword to facsim. edn. discusses Radcliffe's development. Considers character of La Motte.

TC83 Karl, Frederick R. *The Adversary Literature.* NY: Farrar, Straus and Giroux, 1974.

All Gothics are distinguished by the character of the "outsider." Discusses *The Italian*, where the outsider is Schedoni. Points to Radcliffe's use of chiasmus or reversals of fortune. Argues that Radcliffe employs both Gothic and Richardsonian material, mixing Gothic romance with realism. Emily, Ellena, and Adeline are in predicaments similar to that of Clarissa, who is positioned between Lovelace and her family. Radcliffe moves towards social terms: "Implied in her work is a social statement, inchoate as yet, that has as its roots snobbery, vanity, family position, upward mobility, all appearing in the melodramatic terms of the genre" (250).

TC84 Keech, James M. "The Survival of the Gothic Response." *Studies in the Novel* 6 (1974): 130-44.

Brief references to Radcliffe are included in this attempt to define the Gothic not by its trappings and stock characters but by its evocation of fear and foreboding.

TC85 Nettels, Elsa. "The Portrait of a Lady and the Gothic Romance." *South Atlantic Bulletin:* 39 (1974): 73-82.

Examines Radcliffe's influence on Henry James.

TC86 Porte, Joel. "In the Hands of an Angry God: Religious Terror in Gothic Fiction." *The Gothic Imagination: Essays in Dark Ro-*

manticism. Ed. Gary Richard Thompson. Pullman: Washington State UP, 1974. 42-64.

In the context of his argument that the terror of the Gothic novel is theological, Porte briefly discusses *Udolpho* in terms of the sublime. The episode of the dying nun exposes Emily to notions of damnation.

TC87   Rothstein, Eric. "The Lessons of *Northanger Abbey.*" *University of Toronto Quarterly* 44 (1974): 14-30.

Discusses Austen's imitation of Gothic devices, particularly Radcliffe's.

TC88   St. Armand, Barton Levi. "The 'Mysteries' of Edgar Poe: The Quest for a Monomyth in Gothic Literature." *The Gothic Imagination: Essays in Dark Romanticism.* Ed. Gary Richard Thompson. Pullman: Washington State UP, 1974. 65-93.

Deals briefly with Radcliffe, who influenced Poe's "The Assignation" and "The Oval Portrait." Traces the influence of the veil in *Udolpho.* Radcliffe was the first to explore psychological mystery. Cautions that the Gothic was "first and foremost, a fashion, a style, and a mode of interior decoration. That the particular interior being redecorated was human consciousness itself is ancillary to the nature of Gothic as primarily an aesthetic revival which somehow managed to provide Romanticism with its first full set of swaddling clothes" (65).

TC89   Thompson, Gary Richard. Introduction. *The Gothic Imagination: Essays in Dark Romanticism.* Ed. Gary Richard Thompson. Pullman: Washington State UP, 1974. 1-10.

Responds to Radcliffe's assertion in "On the Supernatural in Poetry" that terror, which expands and awakens the spirit, and horror, which constricts it, are opposites. Argues that terror overwhelms the soul from without, while horror comes from "a vast unconscious reservoir of primitive dread" within (4).

TC90   Varma, Devendra P. Introduction. *The Romance of the Forest.* 3 vols. NY: Arno, 1974. 1: xiii-xxix.

Introduction to facsim. edn. Considers the Gothic villain. Positioning Radcliffe between Walpole and the Romantics, argues that *Romance of the Forest* provides a formula for imitators.

TC91   Wilson, Milton. "Travellers' Venice: Some Images for Byron and Shelley." *University of Toronto Quarterly* 43 (1974): 93-120:

Briefly examines Mrs. Thrale's influence on Emily's vision of Venice in *Udolpho,* and, in turn, the influence of Radcliffe's description of Venice on Byron and, more tentatively, on Shelley.

1975

TC92 Berthier, Philippe. "Stendhal, Mme. Radcliffe et l'art du paysage." *Stendhal Club* 17 (1975): 305-307.

Discusses Radcliffe's influence on Stendhal's landscapes.

TC93 Broadwell, Elizabeth P. "The Veil Image in Ann Radcliffe's *The Italian.*" *South Atlantic Bulletin* 40 (1975): 76-87.

In *Udolpho* and *The Italian* Radcliffe develops the veil image as a complex symbolic motif of concealment and revelation.

TC94 Klein, Jürgen. Der gotische Roman und Die Ästhetik des Bösen. Darmstadt: Wissenschaftliche Buchgesellschaft, 1975.

Study of evil in the gothic novel includes brief discussion of Radcliffe.

1976

TC95 Moers, Ellen. *Literary Women.* 1976. NY: Oxford UP, 1985. 125-40.

Influential discussion of the "female Gothic" analyzes Radcliffe's traveling heroine in the novels she classifies as female picaresques. Villains motivate Radcliffe's heroines to action. Suggests that *Udolpho* is shaped on the patterns of women's lives. Montoni is the "shattered mirror image of the impossibly good father . . ." (135). Argues that property is a more important consideration than love in *Udolpho.*

TC96 Price, F.W. "Ann Radcliffe, Mrs. Siddons and the Character of Hamlet." *Notes And Queries* 23 [Vol. 221 of the continuous series] (1976): 164-67.

Discusses the influence of *Hamlet* on Radcliffe in terms of omitted dialogue in *Gaston de Blondeville.*

TC97 Rustowski, Adam. "Convention and Generic Instability of the English Gothic Novel." *Studia Anglica posnanlensia* 8 (1976): 175-87.

Radcliffe is included in attempt to classify Gothic novels.

1977

TC98   Anglo, Michael. *Penny Dreadfuls and Other Victorian Horrors.*
          London: Juniper, 1977.

          Briefly discusses Radcliffe's influence on the genre.

TC99   Arnaud, Pierre. "Les Jardins dans les romans de Mrs.
          Radcliffe." *Autour de l'idée de nature: Histoire des idées et
          civilisation: Pédagogie et divers.* Paris: Didier, 1977: 83-89 (Etudes
          Anglaises 74).

          A study of the garden in *A Sicilian Romance, The Romance of
          the Forest,* and *Udolpho.*

TC100   Doody, Margaret. "Deserts, Ruins and Troubled Waters: Fe-
          male Dreams in Fiction and the Development of the Gothic
          Novel." *Genre* 10 (1977): 529-72.

          In *Athlin and Dunbayne* Osbert is a hero who experiences fear
          and in *The Italian* Vivaldi's experience is more terrifying than
          Ellena's. *A Sicilian Romance* is a nightmare of guilt.

TC101   Foucault, Michel. "The Eye of Power." *Power/Knowledge: Se-
          lected Interviews and Other Writings.* Ed. Colin Gordon. Trans.
          Colin Gordon, Leo Marshall, John Mepham, Kate Soper. 1977.
          NY: Pantheon, 1980. 146-65.

          Radcliffe's terrifying landscapes constitute the "negative of
          the transparency and visibility which it is aimed to establish.
          This reign of 'opinion,' so often invoked at this time, repre-
          sents a mode of operation through which power will be exer-
          cised by virtue of the mere fact of things being known and
          people seen in a sort of immediate, collective and anony-
          mous gaze" (154).

TC102   Garrett, John. "The Eternal Appeal of the Gothic." *The Sphinx*
          2 (1977): 1-7.

          Finds Radcliffe to be both politically and psychologically con-
          servative.

TC103   Holland, Norman N. and Sherman, Leona F. "Gothic Possi-
          bilities." *New Literary History* 8(1977): 279-94. [Rptd. in *Gen-
          der and Reading: Essays on Readers, Texts, and Contexts.* Ed.
          Elizabeth A. Flynn and Patrocinio P. Schweickart. Baltimore:
          Johns Hopkins UP, 1986. 215-33.]

A psychoanalytic examination of the popularity of the Gothic. Dialogue between authors traces their feelings about *Udolpho* to parental models. Stresses the importance of gender in reader response.

TC104 Leranbaum, Miriam. "'Mistresses of Orthodoxy': Education in the Lives and Writings of Late Eighteenth-Century English Women Writers." *Proceedings of the American Philosophical Society* 121 (1977): 281-301.

Examines the education of ten eighteenth-century women including Ann Radcliffe, Clara Reeve, Fanny Burney, Maria Edgeworth, Elizabeth Carter, Elizabeth Montagu, Hester Chapone, Hannah More, Anna Barbauld, and Mary Wollstonecraft.

TC105 Skilton, David. *The English Novel.* London: David and Charles, 1977.

Influenced by Burke's *Sublime and Beautiful,* Radcliffe dramatizes the struggle between reason and irrationality. Compares Radcliffe with Lewis.

TC106 Ware, Malcolm. "The Telescope Reversed: Ann Radcliffe and Natural Scenery." *A Provision of Human Nature: Essays on Fielding and Others in Honor of Miriam Austin Locke.* Ed. Donald Kay. University, Alabama: U of Alabama P, 1977. 169-89.

Strings together quotations to illustrate the picturesque in Radcliffe.

1978

TC107 Albertazzi, Silvia. "Figurazioni oniriche nel romance 'italiano' di Ann Radcliffe." *Spicilegio Moderno* 9 (1978): 146-53.

A study of nightmare imagery in *The Italian* in terms of Ellena and of Radcliffe herself.

TC108 Capone, Giovanna. "'What do I see? . . .': Un paradigma nel romanzo gotico." *Spicilegio Moderno* 10 (1978): 96-114.

Radcliffe's creation of suspense depends on the overactive imaginations of her heroines, who have fantasies of submission.

TC109 Duckworth, Alistair M. "Fiction and Some Uses of the Country House Setting from Richardson to Scott." *Landscape in the*

Gardens and the Literature of Eighteenth-Century England. [Papers read at a Clark Library Seminar 18 March 1978.] Los Angeles: Clark Memorial Library, 1981. 91-128.

Discusses the country house in *Udolpho, Grandison, Humphry Clinker, Pride and Prejudice,* and *The Heart of Midlothian.*

TC110 Hennessy, Brendan. *The Gothic Novel.* Writers and their Work Series. Essex, England: Longman Group, 1978.

Brief consideration of Radcliffe praises her landscape descriptions. *Udolpho* and *The Italian* represent Radcliffe's best novels. Fleetingly discusses Radcliffe's influence on Wordsworth, Byron, Keats, Shelley, Scott, and the Brontës.

TC111 Howells, Coral Ann. *Love, Mystery and Misery: Feeling in Gothic Fiction.* U of London, The Athlone Press, 1978: 28-61. [Revision and expansion of "The Presentation of Emotion in the English Gothic Novels of the Late Eighteenth and Early Nineteenth Centuries." Diss. London U, 1969.]

Radcliffe dramatizes Burke's speculations on sublimity and creates ambivalence by double perspectives. Radcliffe's heroines reveal their emotional range in isolation, as Radcliffe explores feminine anxiety related to loneliness, dependence, and sexual fear. Her distresses form an analogue for the situation of women in the late eighteenth century. Her exaggeration of negative emotions such as fear, misery, and melancholy was the only response available for women wanting to maintain their individuality. Howells discusses Austen's use of *Udolpho* and of *Romance of the Forest* in *Northanger Abbey.* Compares Emily to Austen's Emma, both of whom learn that conclusions based on emotion alone are inadequate—reason must balance feeling. This emphasis situates Radcliffe with eighteenth-century moralists like Richardson and Johnson, and leads to Austen.

TC112 Jones, Lilla Maria Crisafulli. "Parodia e satanismo nel romanzo 'italiano' di Ann Radcliffe." *Spicilegio Moderno* 9 (1978): 136-145.

Describes Schedoni in satanic terms. Ellena's hysteria is a critique of extreme sentiments.

TC113 Lydenberg, Robin. "Gothic Architecture and Fiction: A Survey of Critical Responses." *Centennial Review* 22 (1978): 95-109.

Briefly mentions Radcliffe.

TC114 Rottensteiner, Franz. *The Fantasy Book: The Ghostly, the Gothic, the Magical, the Unreal.* London: Thames and Hudson, 1978.

Brief discussion of Radcliffe.

TC115 Sanna, Vittoria. "La datazione del libro di viaggi di Ann Radcliffe." *Critical Dimensions: English, German and Comparative Literature Essays in Honor of Aurelio Zanco.* Ed. Mario Curreli and Alberto Martino. Cuneo, Italy: SASTE, 1978. 291-312.

Discusses the dating of Radcliffe's *Journey*.

TC116 Zimansky, Curt R. "Shelley's *Wandering Jew*: Some Borrowings from Lewis and Radcliffe." *Studies in English Literature* 18 (1978): 597-609.

Although most of the discussion concerns the influence of *The Monk*, briefly mentions ideas Shelley borrowed from *The Italian*.

1979

TC117 Arnaud, Pierre. "Crime. et châtiment dans le roman romantique." *La Mort, le fantastique, le surnaturel du XVIe siècle à l'époque romantique.* Ed. Michèle Plaisant. Université de Lille III, 1979. 165-71.

Discussion of crime and punishment includes consideration of Radcliffe's works.

TC118 Gilbert, Sandra, and Susan Gubar. *The Madwoman in the Attic: The Woman Writer and the Nineteenth-Century Imagination.* New Haven and London: Yale UP, 1979.

Scattered references to Radcliffe.

TC119 Jarret, David. "A Source for Keats's Magic Casements." *Notes and Queries* 26 (1979): 232-25.

Udolpho influenced *The Eve of St. Agnes* and "Ode to a Nightingale."

TC120 Kelly, Gary. "'A Constant Vicissitude of Interesting Passions': Ann Radcliffe's Perplexed Narratives." *Ariel* 10 (1979): 45-64.

Radcliffe "loosens, relaxes, softens and sentimentalizes" (48) Walpole's form of fiction, lowering the shock level of the narrative and lengthening it out.

TC121 MacAndrew, Elizabeth. *The Gothic Tradition in Fiction.* NY: Columbia UP, 1979.

Compares Schedoni with Lewis's Ambrosio. Radcliffe's heroines develop as a result of being threatened. In *Udolpho* the central Gothic section is framed by the Sentimental. *The Italian* is also structured by contrasted settings. Whereas *Udolpho* has an optimistic resolution, evil is not as clearly domesticated in the conclusion of *The Italian.*

TC122 Rev. by Coral Ann Howells in *English* 30 (1981): 185-90.

TC123 Novak, Maximillian. "The Extended Moment: Time, Dream, History, and Perspective in Eighteenth-Century Fiction." *Probability, Time, and Space in Eighteenth-Century Literature.* Ed. Paula Backscheider. NY: AMS Press, 1979. 141-66.

Argues that the "proper sluggishness" (155) in fiction is a function of such features as multiple perspective, including dreams.

TC124 _____. "Gothic Fiction and the Grotesque." *Novel* 13 (1979): 50-67.

Radcliffe is a major focus of Novak's discussion of the Gothic in terms of the grotesque.

TC125 Pappageorge, Julia di Stefano. "Coleridge's 'Mad Lutanist': A Romantic Response to Ann Radcliffe." *Bulletin of Research in the Humanities* 82 (1979): 222-35.

Argues that Coleridge's "Dejection: An Ode" transforms Radcliffe's lute music in *Udolpho.*

TC126 Poovey, Mary. "Ideology and *The Mysteries of Udolpho*." *Criticism* 21 (1979): 307-30.

A Marxist reading of *Udolpho* that discusses the role of women under patriarchy in the late eighteenth century. Investigates the paradox of sensibility, which restricts women, but at the same time provides them with an arena of power. The inability of Emily's sensibility to arrest Montoni's greed demonstrates the inadequacy of sensibility.

TC127 Tatu, Chantal. "Cris et chuchotements dans *Les Mystères d'Udolphe* d'Anne Radcliffe: Mais à quoi sert le fantastique?" *Caliban* 16 (1979): 87-97.

Discusses Radcliffe's Gothic acoustics.

TC128 Tracy, Ann B. "Gothic, Had-I-But-Known, Damsel-in-Distress." *Murderess Ink: The Better Half of the Mystery.* Ed. Dilys Winn. NY: Workman Publishing, 1979. 14-17.

Radcliffe is briefly mentioned in this fanciful comparison of classic Gothic and later versions.

TC129 Wolff, Cynthia Griffin. "The Radcliffean Gothic Model: A Form for Feminine Sexuality." *Modern Language Studies* 9 (1979): 98-113. [Rptd. in *The Female Gothic.* Ed. Juliann E. Fleenor. Montreal and London: Eden Press, 1983. 207-223.]

Uses analogy of "Devil/Priest" syndrome to explain that women, like men, project their sexual feelings onto two different character types in the opposite sex. This theory provides a foundation for analyzing "The Radcliffean Gothic model," which "has survived virtually intact, attaining almost the status of a cultural myth."

1980

TC130 Blair, David. "Wilkie Collins and the Crisis of Suspense." *Reading the Victorian Novel.* Ed. Ian Gregor. NY: Barnes and Noble, 1980. 32-50.

Briefly considers reader response in *Udolpho.* Readers are disappointed and unconvinced by Radcliffe's "closing flurry of explanations," which replaces the supernatural with the natural, as "the novel seeks to 'tick-off', as it were, all the detail which seemed mysterious . . ." (35).

TC131 Butler, Marilyn. "The Woman at the Window: Ann Radcliffe in the Novels of Mary Wollstonecraft and Jane Austen." *Women and Literature* 1 (1980): 128-48.

Explores the ambivalent attitude of both Wollstonecraft and Austen toward Radcliffe.

TC132 Coleman, William Emmet. *On the Discrimination of Gothicisms.* Gothic Studies and Dissertations Series, ed. Devendra P. Varma. NY: Arno Press, 1980.

Revised version (with a new introduction) of 1970 dissertation.

TC133 Gori, Stefano. "Il brano introduttivo a *The Italian or the Confessional of the Black Penitents* di Ann Radcliffe." *Rivista di letterature moderne e comparate* 33 (1980): 263-69.

Studies the relationship between Radcliffe's introduction and the novel proper. Introductory excerpt.

TC134 Hogle, Jerrold E. "The Restless Labyrinth: Cryptonymy in the Gothic Novel." *Arizona Quarterly* 36 (1980): 330-58.

Examines *Udolpho, The Italian, Otranto, The Monk, Frankenstein, Vathek,* and *Melmoth the Wanderer* to suggest that cryptonymy (crypts supplanting crypts) functions as a controlling principle in the Gothic novel.

TC135 Kahane, Claire. "Gothic Mirrors and Feminine Identity." *Centennial Review* 24 (1980): 43-64.

A feminist and psychoanalytic interpretation of Gothic fiction from Ann Radcliffe to Flannery O'Connor and Shirley Jackson. Argues that the heroine's search for her mother is a central characteristic of the female Gothic. In *Udolpho* Emily encounters precursors/doubles/mother figures in Laurentini and the murdered marchioness, respectively the original owners of Udolpho and of its counterpart, the Chateâu Blanc. Reprinted 1985.

TC136 Lea, Sydney L.W., Jr. *Gothic to Fantastic.* Gothic Studies and Dissertations Series, ed. Devendra P. Varma. NY: Arno Press, 1980.

Published version (unrevised) of 1972 dissertation.

TC137 Lewis, Paul. "Fearful Lessons: The Didacticism of the Early Gothic Novel." *College Language Association Journal* 23 (1980): 470-484.

Moral values diminish the intensity of emotions in Radcliffe. Compares Radcliffe and Lewis.

TC138 May, Leland Chandler. *Parodies of the Gothic Novel.* Gothic Studies and Dissertations Series, ed. Devendra P. Varma. NY: Arno Press, 1980.

Published version (unrevised) of 1969 dissertation.

TC139 Mise, Raymond. *The Gothic Heroine and the Nature of the Gothic Novel.* Gothic Studies and Dissertations Series, ed. Devendra

Varma. NY: Arno Press, 1980.

Published version (unrevised) of 1970 dissertation.

TC140 Platzner, Robert Leonard. *The Metaphyscial Novel in England: The Romantic Phase*. Gothic Studies and Dissertations Series, ed. Devendra P. Varma. NY: Arno Press, 1980.

Published version (unrevised) of 1972 dissertation.

TC141 Punter, David. *The Literature of Terror: A History of Gothic Fictions from 1765 to the Present Day*. NY: Longman, 1980.

A wide-ranging Marxist consideration of the Gothic that includes a lengthy discussion of interconnections among *Udolpho,* which inspired *The Monk,* which in turn, inspired a reaction in the form of *The Italian,* representative of a significant progression. Rejects the conventional distinction between Radcliffe and Lewis as merely a difference between the unexplained and the explained supernatural. Argues, instead, that in all three works the supernatural is not central in and of itself but as a vehicle for larger thematic explorations of the relationship between individual and society. Thus, all three novels are concerned with psychological states, especially sensibility in conflict with useful social activity in the "real" world. Perceptual distortions caused by sensibility are augmented by isolation. The heroines of the three novels are hindered by their repressed passions: "By conceiving of the passions as enemies, the Gothic victim admits a Trojan horse and also loses grip on the facts of his or her own psychology . . ." (82-83). In both Lewis and Radcliffe, the family and the church can become claustrophobic, isolating, and imprisoning. Takes up issues such as the sublime, reader response, city versus country. A version of this chapter appears in Punter's essay in *Romanticism and Ideology* (1981) cited below.

TC142 Rev. by Coral Ann Howells in *English* 30 (1981): 185-90.

TC143 Reddin, Chitra Pershad. *Forms of Evil in the Gothic Novel*. Gothic Studies and Dissertations Series, ed. Devendra P. Varma. NY: Arno Press, 1980.

Published version (unrevised) of 1977 dissertation.

TC144 Reno, Robert Princeton. *The Gothic Visions of Ann Radcliffe and*

and Matthew G. Lewis. Gothic Studies and Dissertations Series, ed. Devendra P. Varma. NY: Arno Press, 1980.

Published version (unrevised) of 1976 dissertation.

TC145 Roberts, Bette B. *The Gothic Romance: Its Appeal to Women Writers and Readers in Late Eighteenth-Century England.* Gothic Studies and Dissertations Series, ed. Devendra P. Varma. NY: Arno Press, 1980.

Published version (unrevised) of 1975 dissertation.

TC146 Ronald, Margaret A. *Functions of Setting in the Novel: From Mrs. Radcliffe to Charles Dickens.* Gothic Studies and Dissertations Series, ed. Devendra P. Varma. NY: Arno Press, 1980.

Published version (unrevised) of 1970 dissertation.

TC147 Sandy, Stephen. *The Raveling of the Novel: Studies in Romantic Fiction from Walpole to Scott.* Gothic Studies and Dissertations Series, ed. Devendra P. Varma. NY: Arno Press, 1980.

Includes discussion of description in *Udolpho.* Published version (revised with a new introduction) of 1963 Harvard dissertation.

TC148 Schroeder, Natalie. "*The Mysteries of Udolpho* and *Clermont*: The Radcliffean Encroachment on the Art of Regina Maria Roche." *Studies in the Novel* 12 (1980): 131-43.

In *Clermont* distinguishes between Rochean and Radcliffean elements by examining characters, landscape, suspense, didacticism and intrigue.

TC149 Sedgwick, Eve Kosofsky. *The Coherence of Gothic Conventions.* Gothic Studies and Dissertations Series, ed. Devendra P. Varma. NY: Arno Press, 1980.

Version of 1975 dissertation with substantial revisions to chapter one. Expanded and revised version published by Methuen in 1986.

TC150 Le Tellier, Robert Ignatius. *An Intensifying Vision of Evil: The Gothic Novel (1764-1820) as a Self-Contained Literary Cycle.* Salzburg: Universität Salzburg, 1980.

Published version of 1977 Rhodes University M.A. thesis. Many references to Radcliffe in this study of the elements (character, setting, plot, world view) of Gothic novels.

TC151 Thomson, John. "Ann Radcliffe's Use of Philippus Van Limborch's *The History of the Inquisition.*" *English Language Notes* 18 (1980): 31-33.

Similarities between *The Italian* and *History of the Inquisition.*

TC152 Van Luchene, Stephen Robert. *Essays in Gothic Fiction.* Gothic Studies and Dissertations Series, ed. Devendra P. Varma. NY: Arno Press, 1980.

Published (unrevised) version of 1973 dissertation.

TC153 Weiss, Fredric. *The Antic Spectre.* Gothic Studies and Dissertations Series, ed. Devendra P. Varma. NY: Arno Press, 1980.

Published (unrevised) version of 1972 dissertation.

TC154 Wilt, Judith. *Ghosts of the Gothic.* Princeton: Princeton UP, 1980.

Considers *The Italian* as "the richest, clearest, most morally intense evocation of the classic Gothic universe" (31). Analyzes Schedoni and his relationship with the Marchesa.

1981

TC155 Beer, Gillian. "'Our Unnatural No-voice': The Heroic Epistle, Pope, and Women's Gothic." 1981. Rptd. in *Modern Essays on Eighteenth-Century Literature.* Ed. Leopold Damrosch, Jr. NY: Oxford UP, 1988. 379-411.

Briefly compares *Eloisa to Abelard* and *The Italian.* In the female Gothic, women authors write even as their heroines are silent. Absolved by inexperience and lack of awareness of responsibility for the trouble she creates, the virginal central consciousness is surrounded by erotic iconography that may not be "owned."

TC156 Durant, David. "Aesthetic Heroism in *The Mysteries of Udolpho.*" *The Eighteenth Century: Theory and Interpretation* 22 (1981): 175-88.

Claims that Radcliffe reworks the Gothic form in *Udolpho.* Examines use of visual imagery to shift focus from morality to aesthetics.

TC157 Punter, David. "Social Relations of Gothic Fiction." In Aers, David, Jonathan Cook, and David Punter. *Romanticism and*

Ideology: Studies in English Writing 1765-1830. London and Boston: Routledge and Kegan Paul, 1981.

A version of Punter's 1980 essay cited above.

TC158 Rogers, Katharine. "Dreams and Nightmares: Male Characters in the Female Novel of the Eighteenth Century." In *Men by Women.* Ed. Janet Todd. NY and London: Holmes and Meier, 1981 (ns 2 of *Women and Literature*): 9-24.

Includes an examination of Radcliffe's male characters: Valancourt and Vivaldi have less self-command than Emily and Ellena; Montoni serves to negate female values. Schedoni is used to illustrate a central theory: "As the heroes in women's novels usually exist to reward the heroine, the villains exist to persecute her innocence" (18).

TC159 Sedgwick, Eve Kosofsky. "The Character in the Veil: Imagery of the Surface in the Gothic Novel." *PMLA* 96 (1981): 255-70.

A poststructuralist reading of *The Italian* and *Udolpho* that deals with surface and depth imagery, characterization, and contagion. Identifies the sexual nature of the veils. Compares Radcliffe to Lewis (*The Monk*). Reprinted in her 1986 Methuen book.

TC160 Thomson, John. "Seasonal and Lighting Effects in Ann Radcliffe's Fiction." *AUMLA: Journal of the Australasian Language and Literature Association* 56 (1981): 191-200.

Scenery in *Romance of the Forest, Udolpho,* and *The Italian.*

TC161 Todd, Janet. "Posture and Imposture: The Gothic Manservant in Ann Radcliffe's *The Italian.*" In *Men by Women.* Ed. Janet Todd. NY and London: Holmes and Meier, 1981 (ns 2 of *Women and Literature*): 25-38.

Considers Paolo as the devoted, loyal, affectionate manservant, the ideal of a female imagination.

TC162 Tracy, Ann B. *The Gothic Novel 1790-1830.* Lexington: UP of Kentucky, 1981.

Includes plot summaries of Radcliffe's novels.

1982

TC163 Anderson, Howard. "Gothic Heroes." *The English Hero, 1660-1800.* Ed. Robert Folkenflik. Newark: U of Delaware P; London and Toronto: Associated University Presses, 1982. 205-221.

Discusses depiction of male protagonists in Walpole, Lewis, and Radcliffe (*Udolpho* and *The Italian*).

TC164 Bayer-Berenbaum, Linda. *The Gothic Imagination: Expansion in Gothic Literature and Art.* Rutherford, NJ: Fairleigh Dickinson UP, 1982.

Scattered references to Radcliffe.

TC165 Durant, David. "Ann Radcliffe and the Conservative Gothic." *Studies in English Literature* 22 (1982): 519-30.

Argues that Radcliffe is a conservative writer whose novels resisted Romanticism: "Radcliffe is not a forerunner of the romantic movement, but the staunch foe of its most salient characteristics" (519). Discusses various thematic and plot devices, as well as treatment of the individual and the family. Radcliffe's heroines enter a "gothic underworld" (525) because their previous protectors disappear: "God finds no one eating the apple; He simply disappears, taking the garden with Him." (521).

TC166 Engel, Leonard. "The Role of the Enclosure in the English and American Gothic Romance." *Essays in Arts and Sciences* 11 (1982): 59-68.

Discusses enclosure as a device to create fear in Horace Walpole's *Otranto*, Ann Radcliffe's *Udolpho*, and Charles Brockden Brown's *Edgar Huntly*.

TC167 Figes, Eva. *Sex and Subterfuge: Women Writers to 1850.* NY: Persea Books, 1982.

Discusses *Udolpho* in terms of its message and scenery. The novel represents "a female equivalent of the male picaresque."

TC168 Haring-Smith, Tori. "The Gothic Novel: A Tale of Terrors Tamed." *Wissenschaftliche Zeitschrift der Wilhelm-Pieck-Universität Rostock* 31 (1982): 49-55.

A discussion of the Gothic in terms of lack of identity, of

passion, and of past crimes. Deals with *The Castle of Otranto* and *The Italian.* In English.

TC169 Modleski, Tania. *Loving with a Vengeance: Mass-Produced Fantasies for Women.* 1982. NY: Methuen, 1984.

Includes brief psychological reading of *Udolpho* in terms of female paranoia, oedipal conflicts, and separation anxiety.

TC170 Morse, David. *Romanticism: A Structural Analysis.* Totowa, NJ: Barnes and Noble, 1982.

Argues that *The Italian* contrasts hypocrisy and innocence. Deals with the cloak and the veil as images of mystification and obscurity. In *The Italian* male domination is thwarted in the person of Schedoni, as the mother-daughter relationship gains significance, ultimately allowing for Ellena's marriage: "In a very real sense Ellena's task in *The Italian* is to lose a father and find a mother" (74).

TC171 Ringe, Donald A. *American Gothic: Imagination and Reason in Nineteenth-Century Fiction.* Lexington: UP of Kentucky, 1982.

Many scattered references to Radcliffe.

TC172 Rogers, Katharine M. *Feminism in Eighteenth-Century England.* Urbana: U of Illinois P, 1982.

Brief comments on Radcliffe's heroines as colorless and feminine, yet strong.

TC173 Stock, R.D. *The Holy and the Daemonic from Sir Thomas Browne to William Blake.* Princeton: Princeton UP, 1982.

Contrasts Schedoni with Vivaldi and Ellena.

1983

TC174 Bellman Nerozzi, Patrizia. "Terrore e consumo: la popolarizzazione del gotico nel romanzo di Ann Radcliffe." *Sheherazade in Inghilterra.* Ed. Patrizia Nerozzi Bellman. Milan: Cisalpino-Goliardica, 1983. 117-41.

Discussion of Radcliffe's popularization of the Gothic considers repetitions of ideas and incidents from one novel to another. Cleverly exploiting the contemporary demand for the sensational, Radcliffe emphasizes the heroine to deal with the equation between sensibility and terror, virtue and fear, encouraging the reader to identify. The issue of feminine sensitivity is introduced by subjecting the heroine to endless ordeals.

TC175 deGategno, Paul J. "Mrs. Ann Radcliffe." *Critical Survey of Long Fiction.* Ed. Frank N. Magill. Englewood Cliffs, NJ: Salem Press, 1983. 6: 2195-2204.

General critical overview of Radcliffe considers her achievements, biography, and influence.

TC176 Fawcett, Mary Laughlin. "*Udolpho*'s Primal Mystery." *Studies in English Literature* 23 (1983): 481-94.

A psychoanalytic reading of *Udolpho* that deals with the primal scene and the relationship to death. Claims possible connections with Blake's *Book of Thel.*

TC177 Grigorescu, Dan. Introduction to *Misterle din Udolpho* by Ann Radcliffe. Budapest: Minerva, 1983.

Unseen.

TC178 Hazen, Helen. *Endless Rapture: Rape, Romance, and the Female Imagination.* NY: Charles Scribner's Sons, 1983.

Brief consideration of Radcliffe.

TC179 Miller, Robin Feuer. "Dostoevsky and the Tale of Terror." *The Russian Novel from Pushkin to Pasternak.* Ed. John Garrard. New Haven: Yale UP, 1983. 103-21.

Deals with Radcliffe, Maturin, and Dostoevsky, who is considered to have elevated the Gothic. From the early nineteenth century, Radcliffe was popular and influential in Russia.

TC180 Nichols, Nina da Vinci. "Place and Eros in Radcliffe, Lewis and Brontë." *The Female Gothic.* Ed. Juliann E. Fleenor. Montreal and London: Eden Press, 1983. 187-206.

Addresses gender differences in treatment of place. For Brontë and Radcliffe, place is a cohesive part of the heroine's character. Lewis isolates and exaggerates place.

TC181 Ronald, Ann. "Terror-Gothic: Nightmare and Dream in Ann Radcliffe and Charlotte Brontë." *The Female Gothic.* Ed. Juliann E. Fleenor. Montreal and London: Eden Press, 1983. 176-86.

Analysis of *Udolpho, The Italian, Jane Eyre,* and *Villette* identifies the psychological structure of most Gothic novels "from wasteland to fairy-tale kingdom and then to sexuality" (179). Discusses the function of terror, travel, sex, dreams and nightmares.

TC182 Varma, Devendra P. "The Starhemberg Collection." *Illustrated London News* 271 (1983): 67-68.

A description of the contemporary Gothic book collection gathered by Louis Starhemberg, Austrian Ambassador to England.

1984

TC183 Bellman Nerozzi, Patrizia. *L'altra faccia del romanzo: creatività destino dell'anti-realismo gotico.* Milan: Cisalpino-Goliardica, 1984.

Includes chapter on the popularization of Radcliffe's novels.

TC184 Flanders, W. Austin. *Structures of Experience: History, Society and Personal Life in the Eighteenth-Century British Novel.* Columbia, SC: U of South Carolina P, 1984.

Examines *The Italian* in terms of the injustice of patriarchal institutions and *Udolpho* in terms of the lack of legal protection for either married or orphaned females.

TC185 Hagstrum, Jean H. "Pictures to the Heart: The Psychological Picturesque in Ann Radcliffe's *The Mysteries of Udolpho.*" *Greene Centennial Studies: Essays Presented to Donald Greene in the Centennial Year of the University of Southern California.* Ed. Paul J. Korshin and Robert R. Allen. Charlottesville: UP of Virginia, 1984. 434-41.

Radcliffe's "pictorialism" consists of relating the emotional and the picturesque.

TC186 Lévy, Maurice. "Le roman gothique, genre anglais." *Europe* 62 (1984): 5-13.

Includes brief references to Radcliffe.

TC187 Murrah, Charles C. "Mrs. Radcliffe's Landscapes: The Eye and the Fancy." *University of Windsor Review* 18 (1984): 7-23.

Scenery in Radcliffe.

TC188 Nollen, Elizabeth. "Ann Radcliffe's *A Sicilian Romance*: A New Source of Jane Austen's *Sense and Sensibility*." *English Language Notes* 22 (1984): 30-37.

Argues that Radcliffe is an overlooked source for Austen's novel. Details the similarities between both sets of sisters, concluding that the proponents of sense and of sensibility are remarkably alike in both novels.

TC189 Tatu, Chantal. "L'Histoire des *Mystères d'Udolphe* en France." *Europe* 659 (1984): 38-53.

Examines the reception of *Udolpho* in France.

1985

TC190 Conger, Syndy. "Fellow Travellers: Eighteenth-Century Englishwomen and German Literature." *Studies in Eighteenth-Century Culture* (ed. O M Brack) 14 (1985): 109-28.

Explores the relationship of eighteenth-century female writers (including Lady Mary Wortley Montagu, Hester Thrale Piozzi, Elizabeth Inchbald, Anna Seward, Anna Barbauld, and Ann Radcliffe) to German culture.

TC191 Conrad, Peter. *The Everyman History of English Literature.* London and Melbourne: J.M. Dent & Sons, 1985.

Brief discussion of Radcliffe's concern with problems generated by indulgences of imagination: "In Mrs Radcliffe's plots, the culprit is always imagination" (392).

TC192 Cottom, Daniel. *The Civilized Imagination: A Study of Ann Radcliffe, Jane Austen, and Sir Walter Scott.* Cambridge, London, NY, New Rochelle, Melbourne, Sydney: Cambridge UP, 1985.

Discusses the "talismanic importance" of Radcliffe's landscape, which allows her to summarize characters and to move the reader past language to a heightened awareness of the surroundings. Landscape is used "to display the delicacy of one's taste." Argues that the dramatic structure of Radcliffe's novels undermines apparent approval of middle-class values.

TC193 Day, William Patrick. *In the Circles of Fear and Desire: A Study of Gothic Fantasy.* Chicago and London: U of Chicago P, 1985.

Considers *Udolpho* with *Uncle Silas* and *Turn of the Screw*, nov-

els that all center on a virtuous heroine imprisoned by patriarchal male authority. *Udolpho* is "a hymn to the power and
value of feminine identity" in which the hero is "reduced to
a cipher" (105). Montoni, who perceives of women as objects, lacks erotic desire. Tormented by Montoni's patriarchal family, Emily goes on to create a feminized family like
the idyllic St. Auberts at the beginning of the novel. If in *The
Italian* the hero is feminized like in *Udolpho*, the masculine
and feminine worlds are much closer together.

TC194 Haggerty, George E. "Fact and Fancy in the Gothic Novel."
       Nineteenth-Century Fiction 39 (1985): 379-91.

       Argues that in the Gothic novel, the nightmare imagery con-
       flicts with and is undermined by realism, yet the fantastical is
       more important than consistency or coherence. Finds that
       "even Ann Radcliffe, the most polished of Gothic writers,
       allows the thrill of the immediate to undermine the overall
       impression of her words" (381).

TC195 Kahane, Claire. "The Gothic Mirror." *The (M)other Tongue:
       Essays in Feminist Psychoanalytic Interpretation.* Ed. Shirley Nelson
       Garner, Claire Kahane, and Madelon Sprengnether. Ithaca:
       Cornell UP, 1985. 334-51.

       Slightly revised version of 1980 article.

TC196 Kostelnick, Charles. "From Picturesque View to Picturesque
       Vision: William Gilpin and Ann Radcliffe." *Mosaic* 18 (1985):
       31-48.

       Examines Radcliffe's use of the picturesque as established by
       William Gilpin. Radcliffe goes beyond Gilpin by inextricably
       connecting picturesque scenes to characters' moral aware-
       ness. Only virtuous characters appreciate nature.

TC197 Magnier, Mireille. "Le Fantastique selon Mrs. Radcliffe."
       Mythes, croyances et religions dans le monde Anglo-Saxon 3 (1985):
       104-111.

       Deals with the fantastic and with Roman Catholicism in
       Radcliffe.

TC198 Napier, Elizabeth. "Ann Radcliffe." *Dictionary of Literary Biog-
       raphy.* Ed. Martin Battestin. Vol. 39, Parts 1+2, *British Novel-
       ists, 1660-1800.* Detroit: Bruccoli Clark Book, 1985. 363-71.

Biographical account with criticism of the novels.

TC199 Rogers, Katharine. "Radcliffe, Ann." *A Dictionary of British and American Women Writers 1660-1800.* Ed. Janet Todd. Totowa, NJ: Rowman and Littlefield, 1985. 262-64.

Brief entry takes up matters like Radcliffe's biography, her villains and heroines, and her contemporary reception.

TC200 Varma, Devendra P. "Ann Radcliffe 1764-1823." *Supernatural Fiction Writers.* Ed. E.F. Bleiler. NY: Charles Scribner's Sons, 1985. 1: 145-51.

Biographical and critical overview and appreciation. Finds *Udolpho* Radcliffe's most popular work, even though *The Italian* is her best. Criticizes Radcliffe's explained supernatural, but praises her scenery and her villains.

1986

TC201 Chard, Chloe. Introduction. *The Romance of the Forest.* NY: Oxford UP, 1986.

Discusses aspects of the novel including the representation of foreign society, of landscape, of oppression and of lack of restraint.

TC202 Cherenkova, N.I. "Tvorcheskii metod A. Radklif i transformatsiia goticheskogo romana." *Vestnik Leningradskogo Universiteta. Seriia istorii, iazyka i literatury* 2 (1986): 50-53.

Deals with the role of terror in the Gothic novel.

TC203 Flaxman, Rhoda L. "Radcliffe's Dual Modes of Vision." *Fetter'd or Free? British Women Novelists, 1670-1815.* Ed. Mary Anne Schofield and Cecilia Macheski. Athens: Ohio UP, 1986. 124-33.

Claims that Radcliffe was "one of the first English novelists to elevate extended, visually oriented landscape description. . . ." (124). Finds her technique cinematic. Describes several of Radcliffe's "word paintings" in *Udolpho.*

TC204 Harwell, Thomas Meade, ed. *The English Gothic Novel.* 4 vols. Salzburg: Institut für Anglistik und Amerikanistik, Universität Salzburg, 1986.

A collection of reprinted essays on the Gothic.

TC205 Hemlow, Joyce, ed. *Fanny Burney: Selected Letters and Journals.*
NY: Oxford UP, 1986. 45n.

Hemlow notes that Radcliffe's name was included in the
subscription list of *Camilla* prefixed to volume 1.

TC206 Kamio, Mitsuo. "Ureijo no uchi to soto: Radcliffe's *The Mysteries of Udolfo." Eibungaku Kenkyu* (Tokyo) 63 (1986): 61-74.

A psychological reading of Gothic conventions in *Udolpho.*

TC207 London, April. "Ann Radcliffe in Context: Marking the
Boundaries of *The Mysteries of Udolpho." Eighteenth-Century Life*
10 (1986): 35-47.

Argues that for Radcliffe, female integrity is based on the
interdependence of value and property. Distinguishes between the "female" trait of imagination and the "male" trait
of reason. *Udolpho* defines the "Augustan ideal," but at the
same time threatens individuality. The Gothic fails to recon-
cile stability with change.

TC208 Restuccia, Frances L. "Female Gothic Writing: 'Under Cover
to Alice.'" *Genre* 18 (1986): 245-66.

Several brief references to Radcliffe in essay on *Northanger
Abbey, The Tenant of Wildfell Hall, Wuthering Heights,* and *Frankenstein.*

TC209 Sedgwick, Eve Kosofsky. *The Coherence of Gothic Conventions.*
NY: Methuen, 1986.

Revised version of dissertation and 1980 Arno book that contains her 1981 PMLA article.

TC210 Spencer, Jane. "Romance and Escape: Ann Radcliffe's *The
Romance of the Forest* (1791)." *The Rise of the Woman Novelist.*
NY and Oxford: Basil Blackwell, 1986. 201-207.

Compares Radcliffe and Sophia Lee to find in Radcliffe a
"more optimistic equation of womanhood with romance"
(201). Discusses *The Romance of the Forest* as "a fantasy of
female power" (201).

TC211 Spender, Dale. "Ann Radcliffe and the Gothic." *Mothers of the
Novel.* London and NY: Routledge and Kegan Paul, 1986.
230-45.

Traces the origin of the Gothic, emphasizing Radcliffe's contribution to the genre. Argues that Radcliffe helped pioneer the Romantic Movement. Stresses debt of Coleridge and other Romantic writers to Radcliffe.

TC212 Wolpers, Theodor. "Schrecken und Vernunft: Die Romane lesende Heldin in Jane Austens *Northanger Abbey*. *Gelebte Literatur in der Literatur*. Ed. Theodor Wolpers. Göttingen: Vandenhoeck & Ruprecht, 1986. 168-84.

Deals with *Northanger Abbey* in terms of *Udolpho*.

1987

TC213 Carter, Margaret L. *Specter or Delusion?: The Supernatural in Gothic Fiction*. Ann Arbor: UMI Research Press, 1987.

Revision of 1986 dissertation includes discussion of the "fantastic-uncanny" in Radcliffe.

TC214 Castle, Terry. "The Spectralization of the Other in *The Mysteries of Udolpho*." *The New Eighteenth Century: Theory, Politics, English Literature*. Ed. Felicity Nussbaum and Laura Brown. NY: Methuen, 1987. 231-53.

A psychoanalytic reading of Radcliffe, arguing that critics repress most of the narrative in *Udolpho* by their "crude focus on the so-called Gothic core" (233). Although Radcliffe has been widely criticized for her explanations of the supernatural, the supernatural is not explained, but rather, "rerouted into the realm of the everyday" (236). Concentrates on Radcliffe's ordinary, domestic scenes to find that she presents a "supernaturalization of everyday life" (234), which "spectralizes" other people, treating them like ghosts. Argues that part of *Udolpho*'s popularity in the late eighteenth century was due to a new anxiety about death. This apprehensiveness led to denial in the form of an obsession with mental images of the dead, including posthumous reunions. This ability to "undo" death also allowed for denial of one's own death. Freud's invention of psychoanalysis is a "perverse elaboration" (252) of Radcliffe's romantic absorptions.

TC215 Conger, Syndy McMillen. "Austen's Sense and Radcliffe's Sensibility." *Gothic* 2 (1987): 16-24.

Northanger Abbey as transformation (rather than denunciation) of Radcliffe's sensibility, itself a transformation of mid-century notions.

TC216 Flaxman, Rhoda L. *Victorian Word-Painting and Narrative: Toward the Blending of Genres.* Ann Arbor: UMI Research Press, 1987.

Discusses Radcliffe's landscapes in *Udolpho.*

TC217 Hennelly, Mark M., Jr. "'The Slow Torture of Delay': Reading *The Italian.*" *Studies in the Humanities* 14 (1987): 1-17.

Radcliffe's use of the Inquisition provides a "penitential ordeal" (2) not only for the characters, but also for the reader. Discusses Radcliffe's confessional mode.

TC218 Kadish, Doris Y. *The Literature of Images.* New Brunswick and London: Rutgers UP, 1987.

In both *Udolpho* and *Frankenstein,* the oppostitional structure of the sublime and beautiful exemplifies confinement and liberation, allowing for alternative ways of depicting women and nature.

TC219 Magnier, Mireille. *"L'Italien; Ou, Le Confessionnal des pénitents noirs* réussite majeure de Mrs. Radcliffe." *Mythes, croyances et religions dans le monde Anglo-Saxon* 5 (1987): 113-117.

Discusses Radcliffe's narrative method.

TC220 Napier, Elizabeth R. *The Failure of Gothic: Problems of Disjunction in an Eighteenth-Century Literary Form.* Oxford: Clarendon Press, 1987.

Udolpho valorizes suffering and melancholy, even as it devalues sensibility, elevating fortitude. Emily's imprisonment at Udolpho tests her qualities of self-command, restraint, and endurance, qualities that encourage passivity. In this scheme, heroism involves suffering. Radcliffe suggests that loss (which becomes desirable) is essential for elevated feeling. With obvious authorial endorsement, Emily clings to decorum and morality in non-social and non-moral situations, avoiding action. Her reluctance to involve others in her predicaments leads to extreme isolation. Emily's fortitude, which isolates her, becomes masochistic. Deals with the disjunction of the moral and the dramatic in *The Italian.* If Schedoni's role is theatrical, his power resides in his inwardness.

TC221 Rev. by Margaret Carter in *Eighteenth-Century Studies* 21 (1988): 364-67.

TC222 Simpson, Mark S. "Aleksandr Bestuzhev-Marlinskii and the Gothic Novel in Russia." *Russian, Croatian and Serbian, Czech and Slovak, Polish Literature* 22 (1987): 343-58.

Compares Radcliffe to Bestuzhev.

TC223 Varma, Devendra P. Introductions. *The Complete Novels of Mrs. Ann Radcliffe.* London: The Folio Society, 1987.

Published on the anniversary of Radcliffe's 1787 marriage, the texts of all six novels are based on first editions. With six short critical introductions by Devendra P. Varma.

TC224 Varnado, S.L. *Haunted Presence: The Numinous in Gothic Fiction.* Tuscaloosa and London: U of Alabama P, 1987.

Discusses Radcliffe's "instinctive feeling for the numinous" (29) in terms of the sublime as articulated by Burke.

1988

TC225 Magnier, Mireille. "Le Moine Schemoli et la famille Montorio." *Mythes, croyances et religions dans le monde Anglo-Saxon* 6 (1988): 59-70.

Deals with Maturin's *Fatal Revenge* and Radcliffe's *Italian.*

TC226 Sage, Victor. *Horror Fiction in the Protestant Tradition.* NY: St. Martin's Press, 1988.

Discusses rational explanations of the supernatural in *Udolpho* in terms of religion. Analysis of *The Italian* concerns the ambiguity of testimony.

TC227 Timpane, John. "Ann Ward Radcliffe." *An Encyclopedia of British Women Writers.* Ed. Paul and June Schlueter. NY and London: Garland, 1988. 373-74.

Brief biographical and critical entry. Influence of Sophia Lee's *The Recess* allowed Radcliffe to reject realism in her "powerful explorations of female fantasy" (373).

TC228 Wiesenfarth, Joseph. *Gothic Manners and the Classic English Novel.* Madison: U of Wisconsin P, 1988.

Brief, negative assessment of Radcliffe finds that her "reach exceeds her grasp: she searches for sublimity but finds confusion" (5). In Radcliffe, the heroine and her imagination

are the center of attention. The villain finds her cash more attractive than her virtue.

1989

TC229 Benedict, Barbara M. "Pictures of Conformity: Sentiment and
Structure in Ann Radcliffe's Style." *Philological Quarterly* 68
(1989): 363-77.

The style of *Udolpho* frames imaginative, emotional, fearful, and
sentimental expressions within rationalistic language. Emily's
misreading of pictures is an important plot device.

TC230 Conger, Syndy M. "Sensibility Restored: Radcliffe's Answer to
Lewis's *The Monk*." *Gothic Fictions: Prohibition/Transgression*. Ed.
Kenneth W. Graham. NY: AMS, 1989. 113-49.

The emphasis on psychological response in *The Italian* provides
a "sustained counterstatement" (129) to the emphasis on the
physical and the sensory in *The Monk*. A reaction to Lewis's "sensory bombardment" (130), Radcliffe's sensory deprivation and
obscurity allow for psychological experience. Argues against critics who present Radcliffe as a foe of sensibility (like Austen) to
find that Radcliffe is a resolute defender of this ethos.

TC231 Ellis, Kate Ferguson. *The Contested Castle: Gothic Novels and the
Subversion of Domestic Ideology*. Urbana and Chicago: U of Illinois
P, 1989.

Considers Radcliffe's novels as didactic. Deals with economic
matters in *Udolpho*, considered to be Radcliffe's most female-centered novel. *The Italian* is Radcliffe's least female-centered novel
because the focus is on the developing consciousness of the
villain rather than the heroine.

TC232 Rev. by Mary O'Connor in *Eighteenth-Century Fiction* 4 (1992):
367-68.

TC233 Graham, Kenneth W. "Emily's Demon-Lover: The Gothic Revolution and *The Mysteries of Udolpho*." *Gothic Fictions: Prohibition/
Transgression*. Ed. Kenneth W. Graham. NY: AMS, 1989. 163-71.

Radcliffe attenuates situations by delaying climaxes. Montoni's image as a powerful demon is a product of Emily's imagination.

In actuality Montoni is an impotent failure, who at once attracts and repulses Emily. Finds tension between the domestic world of St. Aubert and Valancourt and the passionate, smouldering world of Montoni. Radcliffe is revolutionary in her exploration and pushing of the boundaries of convention.

TC234 Haggerty, George E. *Gothic Fiction/Gothic Form.* University Park, Pennsylvania and London: Pennsylvania State UP, 1989.

Chapter 1 is a revised version of Haggerty's 1985 article. Other brief considerations of Radcliffe deal with her use of suspense and her manipulation of picturesque setting.

TC235 Howells, Coral Ann. "The Pleasure of the Woman's Text: Ann Radcliffe's Subtle Transgressions in *The Mysteries of Udolpho* and *The Italian*." *Gothic Fictions: Prohibition/Transgression.* Ed. Kenneth W. Graham. NY: AMS, 1989. 151-62.

A Barthesian reading of Radcliffe, arguing that her works contain eccentric moments in which contradictory codes meet. Radcliffe subverts the "hero-rescues-heroine" plot by leaving her heroines isolated and harrassed. Valancourt does not save Emily. Ellena's rescue is also arbitrary. Similar abberations occur in Emily's obsession with Montoni and the male power that he represents. Although Montoni is only interested in Emily for financial reasons, he becomes ". . . the blank on to which she can project all her own desires and fears and still feel viruous and persecuted" (156). Happy endings mute the challenge to convention.

TC236 Macdonald, D. L. "Bathos and Repetition: The Uncanny in Radcliffe." *Journal of Narrative Technique* 19 (1989): 197-204.

Invokes Todorov to deal with *Udolpho* in terms of the uncanny and the unspeakable. Radcliffe's explained supernatural is bathetic.

TC237 McWhir, Anne. "The Gothic Transgression of Disbelief: Walpole, Radcliffe and Lewis." *Gothic Fictions: Prohibition/Transgression.* Ed. Kenneth W. Graham. NY: AMS, 1989. 29-47.

Argues that Gothic novels encourage both scepticism and excessive emotional reactions. Discusses anti-Catholicism in the Gothic novel. Finds that Radcliffe discriminates between "belief and the suspension of disbelief" (39).

TC238 Madoff, Mark S. "Inside, Outside, and the Gothic Locked-

Room Mystery." *Gothic Fictions: Prohibition/Transgression.* Ed. Kenneth W. Graham. NY: AMS, 1989. 49-62.

Discusses architectural space as metaphor in *Udolpho* and *The Monk.* The locked room or "inside," where Radcliffe's characters undergo transformations, consists of a realm that is chaotic, dangerous, and passionate, whereas the "outside" is orderly, secure, civilized, repressed, and rational. Protagonists move between inside and outside, "between experience and innocence, between danger and security, between chaos and order, between the subconscious and the conscious, between anarchy and civilization, between licence and repression" (49).

TC239 Magnier, Mireille. "Croyances médiévales dans *Gaston de Blondeville* (1826)." *Mythes, croyances et religions dans le monde Anglo-Saxon* 7 (1989): 125-132.

Examines *Gaston* in terms of beliefs in the Middle Ages.

TC240 Roberts, Bette B. "The Horrid Novels: *The Mysteries of Udolpho* and *Northanger Abbey.*" *Gothic Fictions: Prohibition/Transgression.* Ed. Kenneth W. Graham. NY: AMS, 1989. 89-111.

The horrid novels listed in *Northanger Abbey* point to the superiority of Radcliffe's novels.

TC241 Satz, Martha. "Radcliffe, Ann." *British Women Writers: A Critical Reference Guide.* Ed. Janet Todd. NY: Continuum, 1989. 550-552.

Biographical sketch with brief summaries of *Udolpho* and *The Italian.*

TC242 Shor, IU. V. Stilisticheskie osobennosti angliiskogo goticheskogo romana: na materiale romana A. Radklif *Udol'fskie tainy. Analiz stilei zarubezhnoi khudozhestvennoi i nauchnoi literatury.* (Leningrad) 6 (1989): 57-65.

Bases analysis of stylistic peculiarities of English Gothics on *Udolpho.*

TC243 Spacks, Patricia Meyer. "Female Orders of Narrative: Clarissa and The Italian." *Rhetorics of Order/Ordering Rhetorics in English Neoclassical Literature.* Ed. J. Douglas Canfield and J. Paul Hunter. Newark: U of Delaware P, 1989. 158-72.

Deals with interpretation in *The Italian.* More fully worked out in Spacks' 1990 book.

TC244 Todd, Janet. "'The Great Enchantress': Ann Radcliffe." *The Sign of Angellica: Women, Writing and Fiction 1660-1800*. London: Virago; NY: Columbia UP, 1989. 253-72.

A wide-ranging general discussion of Radcliffe encompassing biography as well as technique. Takes up such matters as her gothic architecture, poetic descriptions, sentimentalism, didacticism, and characterization.

TC245 _____. "Woman as Artist in the Late Eighteenth Century." *Studies on Voltaire and the Late Eighteenth Century* 264 (1989): 1157-59.

Abstract of conference paper that considers Ann Radcliffe, Fanny Burney, and Charlotte Smith in terms of internal conflicts over the status of English women writers.

TC246 Wolf, Werner. "Schauerroman und Empfindsamkeit: Zur Beziehung zwischen *Gothic Novel* und empfindsamem Roman in England." *Anglia* 107 (1989): 1-33.

Compares sentimental and Gothic novels by considering *Udolpho, Pamela, Frankenstein,* and *Melmoth the Wanderer.*

1990

TC247 Blain, Virginia, Patricia Clements and Isobel Grundy, eds. "Radcliffe, Ann." *The Feminist Companion to Literature in English*. New Haven and London: Yale UP, 1990. 884.

Brief biographical-critical entry.

TC248 Blodgett, Harriet. "Emily Vindicated: Ann Radcliffe and Mary Wollstonecraft." *Weber Studies* 7 (Fall 1990): 48-61.

Wollstonecraft may have influenced Radcliffe.

TC249 DeLamotte, Eugenia C. *Perils of the Night: A Feminist Study of the Nineteenth-Century Gothic*. NY: Oxford UP, 1990.

Radcliffe's double message is: "Rejoice, young ladies—you are tremendously powerful, but watch out—you are defenseless" (34). Unlike Richardson's heroines, Radcliffe's do not know what threatens them: "In Radcliffe's romances, not knowing is a source of terror, but terror is also a source of not knowing" (43).

TC250 Frank, Frederick S. *Through the Pale Door: A Guide to and* *through the American Gothic.* London and Westport, CT: Greenwood Press, 1990.

Critical synopses include comments on Radcliffe's influence.

TC251 Lecercle, Ann. "L'Inscription du regard." *Du Fantastique en littérature.* Ed. Max Duperray. Aix-en-Provence: Univ. de Provence, 1990. 77-93.

Compares *Udolpho* to Poe's "Oval Portrait."

TC252 Spacks, Patricia Meyer. *Desire and Truth: Functions of Plot in Eighteenth-Century English Novels.* Chicago: U of Chicago P, 1990.

Extended discussion of *The Italian* and *Udolpho* designates Radcliffe's plots as "daughters' plots" because they "accord due weight to the daughter's predictable system of values, her stress on attachment" and, "allowing attachment to triumph, such plots covertly demystify the father's force" (160). Radcliffe's double plots coincide with Burkean distinctions between the sublime and the beautiful. Interpretation becomes a major part of the action. Examines the poetry in *Udolpho* in terms of the plot of the narrative as a whole.

1991

TC253 Adickes, Sandra. *The Social Quest: The Expanded Vision of Four Women Travelers in the Era of the French Revolution.* NY: Peter Lang, 1991.

Published version of dissertation includes one of the few recent discussions of Radcliffe's travel writing.

TC254 Bernstein, Stephen. "Form and Ideology in the Gothic Novel." *Essays in Literature* 18 (1991): 151-65.

Discusses the ideology of the gothic novel in terms of Walpole, Radcliffe, Lewis, and Maturin.

TC255 Bruce, Donald Williams. "Ann Radcliffe and the Extended Imagination." *Contemporary Review* 258 (1991): 300-308.

Discursively touches on Radcliffe's heroines, landscapes, morbid sensibility, and characterization of Schedoni.

TC256 Ellison, John A. "Sublime Scenes and Horrid Novels: Milestones along the Road to Middle-Earth." *Mallorn* 28 (1991): 23-28.

Imaginative attempt to "update" *Northanger Abbey* includes comparison of Radcliffe and Tolkien.

TC257 Miles, Robert. *Gothic Writing 1764-1850.* Pinter, 1991.

Unseen. Not available in the U.S. See Miles (1993)..

TC258 Morrison, Paul. "Enclosed in Openness: *Northanger Abbey* and the Domestic Carceral." *Texas Studies in Literature and Language* 33 (1991): 1-23.

Discusses the relationship between *Northanger Abbey* and *Udolpho.*

TC259 Ross, Deborah. *The Excellence of Falsehood: Romance, Realism, and Women's Contribution to the Novel.* Lexington: The UP of Kentucky, 1991.

Compares *The Italian* with Burney's *Cecilia.*

TC260 Taylor, Michael. "Reluctant Romancers: Self-Consciousness and Derogation in Prose Romance." *English Studies in Canada* 17 (1991): 89-106.

Compares the attitude towards prose romance in Ann Radcliffe's *Udolpho*, Sir Philip Sidney's *Acadia*, Sir Walter Scott's *Guy Mannering*, and Henry James's *The American.* Radcliffe's "complacency as a romancer is . . . based on the paradoxical intention of her romance to warn its readers, through the fog of romantic titillation, to eschew the romance sensibility" (95).

1992

TC261 Barker-Benfield, G.J. *The Culture of Sensibility: Sex and Society in Eighteenth-Century Britain.* Chicago and London: U of Chicago P, 1992.

Briefly discusses the importance of sensibility in Radcliffe's work, including fleeting observations on her sentimentalization of trees and insects and her feminization of Valancourt.

TC262 Derry, Stephen. "Harriet Smith's Reading." *Persuasions* 14 (1992): 70-72.

Discusses reference to *Romance of the Forest* in *Emma.*

TC263 Geary, Robert F. *The Supernatural in Gothic Fiction: Horror,*

Belief, and Literary Change. Lewiston, NY: The Edwin Mellen Press, 1992.

Discusses *Udolpho* and *The Italian* in terms of the numinous.

TC264   Greenfield, Susan C. "Veiled Desire: Mother-Daughter Love and Sexual Imagery in Ann Radcliffe's *The Italian.*" *The Eighteenth Century: Theory and Interpretation* 33 (1992): 73- 89.

Studies the sexual nature of veil imagery in *The Italian* to argue that Ellena's relationships with maternal figures are homoerotic.

TC265   Heller, Tamar. *Dead Secrets: Wilkie Collins and the Female Gothic.* New Haven: Yale UP, 1992.

Version of 1988 dissertation discusses mothers and daughters in the Radcliffean Gothic. In *Udolpho* after the death of her mother, Emily's discovery of "the powerlessness of a series of mother substitutes encodes the plot that feminist critics have identified as 'matrophobia,' or the daughter's fear of becoming as powerless and oppressed as the mother" (19).

TC266   Massé, Michelle. *In the Name of Love: Women, Masochism, and the Gothic.* Ithaca: Cornell UP, 1992.

Scattered references to Radcliffe.

TC267   Milbank, Alison. *Daughters of the House: Modes of the Gothic in Victorian Fiction.* NY: St. Martin's Press, 1992.

Discusses Radcliffe's "female Gothic" and relationships between Radcliffe and other writers such as Wilkie Collins, the Brontës, Sheridan le Fanu, and, most extensively, Charles Dickens.

TC268   Richter, David H. "From Medievalism to Historicism: Representations of History in the Gothic Novel and Historical Romance." *Studies in Medievalism* 4 (1992): 79-104.

Includes discussion of historical settings in *Athlin and Dunbayne, Udolpho, The Italian*, and *Gaston.*

TC269   Snyder, William. "Mother Nature's Other Natures: Landscape in Women's Writing, 1770-1830." *Women's Studies* 21 (1992): 143-62.

An analysis of the use of landscape by Dorothy Wordsworth, Jane Austen, and Ann Radcliffe. *The Italian* is an "exploration of sexuality on a field of spirituality, with landscape playing a dominating role in the narrative" (159).

TC270 Turner, Cheryl. *Living by the Pen: Women Writers in the Eighteenth Century.* London and NY: Routledge, 1992.

Scattered references to Radcliffe.

TC271 Winter, Kari. "Sexual/Textual Politics of Terror: Writing and Rewriting the Gothic Genre in the 1790s." *Misogyny in Literature.* Ed. Katherine Ackley. NY: Garland, 1992. 89-103.

Compares Lewis and Radcliffe in terms of male and female Gothic. The male Gothic "lingered over horrible spectacles of sexual violence, gore, and death, locating evil in the other." The female Gothic is concerned with the horror and terror of the familiar. Radcliffe finds the source of evil in human beings, whereas Lewis finds it in the supernatural. Radcliffe's Gothic expresses the violence and injustice of patriarchal society, while Lewis's Gothic inscribes the dominant ideology.

1993

TC272 Berglund, Birgitta. *Woman's Whole Existence: The House as an Image in the Novels of Ann Radcliffe, Mary Wollstonecraft and Jane Austen.* Lund, Sweden: Lund UP, 1993.

Published version of thesis discusses Radcliffe's use of architectutral structure and her theme of imprisonment.

TC273 Mellor, Anne K. *Romanticism and Gender.* NY and London: Routledge, 1993.

Discusses Radcliffe's use of the sublime, arguing that, for Radcliffe, "the deepest terror aroused by the masculine sublime originates in the exercise of patriarchal authority within the home" (93).

TC274 Milbank, Alison. Introduction. *A Sicilian Romance.* NY, Oxford, etc.: Oxford UP, 1993.

Discusses the mother who is absent from the center of the novel and the effect of the sublime.

TC275 Miles, Robert. *Gothic Writing 1750-1820.* London and NY: Routledge, 1993.

Discusses interiority in Radcliffe. Considers *The Italian* in terms of *The Monk*.

TC276 Wolstenholme, Susan. *Gothic (Re)visions: Writing Women as Readers.* Albany: State U of New York P, 1993.

Expanded and revised version of 1989 dissertation. Chapter on *The Italian* deals with "gendering the spectator," repetitions, doublings, repression and storytelling.

1994

TC277 Haggerty, George E. "Sensibility and Sexuality in *The Romance of the Forest.*" *The Critical Response to Ann Radcliffe.* Ed. Deborah D. Rogers. London and Westport, CT: Greenwood Press, 1994. 8-16.

Studies the role of Theodore to argue that *Romance of the Forest* articulates a female principle that rejects patriarchal domination.

TC278 Howard, Jacqueline. *Reading Gothic Fiction: A Bakhtinian Approach.* NY: Oxford UP, 1994.

Discusses *Udolpho, The Monk, Northanger Abbey,* and *Frankenstein* from the perspective of Bakhtinian theory.

TC279 Michasiw, Kim Ian. "Ann Radcliffe and the Terrors of Power." *Eighteenth-Century Fiction* 6 (1994): 327-46.

Discusses power relationships in Radcliffe's novels.

TC280 Scott, Linda Kane. "The Wages of Sin in *Udolpho.*" *The Critical Response to Ann Radcliffe.* Ed. Deborah D. Rogers. London and Westport, CT: Greenwood Press, 1994. 30.

Note on religion in *Udolpho.*

TC281 Yurchuk, Maryanne. "Emotion and Reason in *The Romance of the Forest.*" *The Critical Response to Ann Radcliffe.* Ed. Deborah D. Rogers. London and Westport, CT: Greenwood Press, 1994. 7.

Discusses Radcliffe's protofeminism in terms of the attempt to balance the emotional and rational.

1995

TC282 Rogers, Deborah D., Ed. and Intro. *Two Gothic Classics by Women* [*The Italian and Northanger Abbey*]. NY: Dutton Signet, 1995.

Introduction discusses Radcliffe's female Gothic in terms of her explained supernatural, landscape descriptions, feminized heroes, arresting villains, persecuted (yet independent) heroines, and female kinship relations, especially the mother-daughter bond. Austen appropriates Radcliffe's dislocation of traditional Gothic elements.

7

FULL-LENGTH WORKS (F)

1826

F1 [Talfourd, Sir Thomas Noon (Serjeant Talfourd)]. "Memoir of the Life and Writings of Mrs. Radcliffe." Prefixed to *Gaston.* 1826. See E131.

Earliest full biography forms the basis for all others.

1911

F2 Brey, Joseph. *Die Naturschilderungen in den Romanen und Gedichten der Mrs. Ann Radcliffe. . . .* Nürnberg: Körn, 1911.

Published version of dissertation uses extensive quotation of Radcliffe's novels to examine her treatment of nature.

1920

F3 McIntyre, Clara Frances. *Ann Radcliffe in Relation to her Time.* New Haven: Yale UP, 1920.

Published version of Yale dissertation examines Radcliffe, a transitional figure, through the lens of her contemporaries. Studies their opinion of her personal life, her works, her influence on other authors, and her place in the development of the novel. Radcliffe's most important contribution to the novel is not thematic, but structural. Argues that Radcliffe fails to individualize her characters. Useful bibliography contains some mistakes.

1926

F4   Wieten, Alida Alberdina Sibbellina. *Mrs. Radcliffe—Her Rela-
           tion towards Romanticism.* Amsterdam: H.J. Paris, 1926.

           Published version of dissertation. After a brief biographical
           sketch, discusses Radcliffe's portrayal of lovers to find their
           feelings "delicate and refined." In contrast, Radcliffe's vil-
           lains experience the old order of sensual love (for example,
           in *Tom Jones*). Concentrates on the poems interspersed in the
           novels rather than on the novels themselves. Uses examples
           from Radcliffe's work to posit her views on many issues, from
           social conditions to architecture. Appendix on false attribu-
           tions.

1951

F5   Grant, Aline. *Ann Radcliffe: A Biography.* Denver: Alan Swal-
           low, 1951.

           The most complete and detailed biography of Radcliffe in
           English. This account is undocumented, although sources
           ostensibly include town and county records, a wide range of
           correspondence, and Talfourd's Memoir. Interspersed with
           extensive passages from Radcliffe's journals (taken from
           Talfourd), this embellished biography is full of speculation.

1970

F6   Spina, Georgio. *L'epoca d'oro dei "Tales of Terror": Ann Radcliffe.*
           Genova, Italy: Fratelli Bozzi, 1970.

           Criticism of Radcliffe's novels contains comparisons with other
           Gothic novelists. In Italian.

1972

F7   Murray, E.B. *Ann Radcliffe.* NY: Twayne, 1972.

           Biographical and critical introduction to Radcliffe, who both
           aided and restrained the explosion into Romanticism in the
           1790's. Her major contribution to the development of the
           novel is psychological suspense. Argues that Radcliffe devel-
           ops the eighteenth-century novel of sensibility like Walpole,
           who combined the theme of parental tyranny, a sentimental
           cliché, with the ghost story. Citing Milton and the Graveyard

Poets as sources for Gothic tradition, provides background for the Gothic form, especially its use of our "instinctive fear of the supernatural." Outlines debate on the explained supernatural in Gothic novels. Separate chapters discuss the novels.

1976

F8 Arnaud, Pierre. *Ann Radcliffe et le fantastique: Essai de psychobiographie.* Paris: Aubier Montaigne, 1976.

Psycho-biography with summaries of the novels. Relates Radcliffe's works to her neuroses, speculating about her novels in terms of her repression and her sexual conflicts.

1980

F9 Durant, David Sedgwick, Jr. *Ann Radcliffe's Novels: Experiments in Setting.* Gothic Studies and Dissertations Series, ed. Devendra P. Varma. NY: Arno Press, 1980.

Revision of 1971 dissertation.

F10 Garrett, John. *Gothic Strains and Bourgeois Sentiments in the Novels of Mrs. Ann Radcliffe and her Imitators.* Gothic Studies and Dissertations Series, ed. Devendra P. Varma. NY: Arno Press, 1980.

Published version (unrevised) of 1973 dissertation.

F11 Heller, Lynne Epstein. *Ann Radcliffe's Gothic Landscape of Fiction and the Various Influences upon It.* Gothic Studies and Dissertations Series, ed. Devendra P. Varma. NY: Arno Press, 1980.

Published version (unrevised) of 1971 dissertation.

F12 Sherman, Leona F. *Ann Radcliffe and the Gothic Romance: A Psychoanalytic Approach.* Gothic Studies and Dissertations Series, ed. Devendra P. Varma. NY: Arno Press, 1980.

Published version (unrevised) of 1975 dissertation.

F13 Smith, Nelson Charles. *The Art of Gothic: Ann Radcliffe's Major Novels.* Gothic Studies and Dissertations Series, ed. Devendra P. Varma. NY: Arno Press, 1980.

Revision of 1967 dissertation includes new introduction.

F14   Stoler, John Andrew. *Ann Radcliffe: The Novel of Suspense and Terror.* Gothic Studies and Dissertations Series, ed. Devendra P. Varma. NY: Arno Press, 1980.

Published version (unrevised) of 1972 dissertation.

F15   Swigart, Ford Harris, Jr. *A Study of the Imagery in the Gothic Romances of Ann Radcliffe.* Gothic Studies and Dissertations Series, ed. Devendra P. Varma. NY: Arno Press, 1980.

Revision of 1966 dissertation includes short supplementary bibliography.

F16   Tompkins, J.M.S. *Ann Radcliffe and her Influence on Later Writers.* Gothic Studies and Dissertations Series, ed. Devendra P. Varma. NY: Arno Press, 1980.

Published (unrevised) version of 1921 M.A. thesis. Foreword by Maurice Lévy; introduction by Devendra P. Varma. Deals with contemporary influences on Radcliffe. Analyzes her landscapes and her influence on other writers.

1985

F17   Sanna, Vittoria. *I romanzi gotici di Ann Radcliffe.* Pisa: ETS, 1985.

Unseen.

1987

F18   Scott, Eileen Margaret. *Pastoral Dreams and Gothic Nightmares: Pastoral and Ann Radcliffe: An Examination of* The Romance of the Forest *and* The Mysteries of Udolpho *in Relation to Eighteenth-Century Pastoral Poetry.* Newcastle upon Tyne: University of Newcastle upon Tyne, 1987.

Unseen. Unavailable in the United States.

1991

F19   Blaszak, Marek. *Ann Radcliffe's Gothic Romances and the Romantic Revival.* Opole: Wyzsza Szkola Pedagogiczna im. Powstancow Slaskich w Opolu, 1991.

In English. Considers Radcliffe as a forerunner of Romanticism. Deals with Radcliffe's "black character" and the Byronic hero, her concept of romantic love, her attitude towards nature, and her creation of mystery, suspense, and dramatic psychology.

1994

F20   Rogers, Deborah D., ed. *The Critical Response to Ann Radcliffe.* London and Westport, CT: Greenwood Press, 1994.

A collection of almost one hundred documents, including contemporary reviews, letters, and diary entries, the most important critical assessments, and several new pieces. An introduction provides an extensive overview of the critical response to Radcliffe from the publication of her first novel in 1789 to the present.

8

DISSERTATIONS (D)

1962

D1   Hudson, Randolph Hoyt. "Hence, Vain Deluding Joys: The Anatomy of Eighteenth-Century English Gothicism." Diss. Stanford U, 1962. *DA* 22 (1962): 4344.

This attempt to define the Gothic in terms of the pastoral/ anti-pastoral includes discussion of Radcliffe.

1963

D2   Pound, Edward Fox. "The Influence of Burke and the Psychological Critics on the Novels of Ann Radcliffe." Diss. U of Washington, 1963. *DA* 25 (1964): 1198.

Examines *Udolpho* as the culmination of Radcliffe's use of contemporary psychological and aesthetic theory.

1966

D3   Swigart, Ford Harris, Jr. "A Study of the Imagery in the Gothic Romances of Ann Radcliffe." Diss. U of Pittsburgh, 1966. *DA* 27 (1967): 2509A-10A.

Analyzes many images including: fire, art, light, animals, knives, prisons, music, softness, storms, death, ghosts, magic, religion, poison, and illness. Concludes that Radcliffe's images are general, conventional, and functional. Published (revised) in 1980.

1967

D4   Keebler, Lee Edward. "Ann Radcliffe: A Study in Achieve-
ment." Diss. U of Wisconsin, 1967. *DA* 28 (1968): 3145A.

Argues for Radcliffe's progressive improvement.

D5   Smith, Nelson Charles. "The Art of Gothic: Ann Radcliffe's
Major Novels." Diss. U of Washington, 1967. *DA* 29 (1968):
240A-41A.

Focusing on *Udolpho, Romance of the Forest,* and *The Italian,*
discusses Radcliffe's heroines in terms of critique of sensibility. Radcliffe uses Gothic style to censure its exaggerations.
Published (revised) in 1980.

1969

D6   Howells, Coral Ann. "The Presentation of Emotion in the
English Gothic Novels of the Late Eighteenth and Early Nineteenth Centuries." Diss. London U, 1969.

Early version of Howells' 1979 book, *Love, Mystery, and Misery.*

D7   May, Leland Chandler. "Parodies of the Gothic Novel." Diss.
Oklahoma State U, 1969. *DAI* 31 (1971): 4128A. Published
(unrevised) in 1980.

Deals with Radcliffe in chapters on Jane Austen's *Northanger
Abbey* and on Eaton Stannard Barrett's *The Heroine.*

1970

D8   Coleman, William Emmet. "On the Discrimination of
Gothicisms." Diss. City U of New York, 1970. *DAI* 31 (1970):
2871A.

Argues for an all-embracing definition of the Gothic. Considers Radcliffe in discussion of Gothicism of sensibility. Revised version published in 1980.

D9   Mise, Raymond W. "The Gothic Heroine and the Nature of
the Gothic Novel." Diss. U of Washington, 1970. *DAI* 31
(1971): 3513A.

Emphasizing *Udolpho, The Italian,* and *The Monk,* discusses
the heroine in terms of her familiy relationships, journey,
confinement, incest, and marriage. Chastity and sensibility

are connected to the heroine's fear and anxiety. Published (unrevised) in 1980.

D10 Reilly, Donald Thomas. "The Interplay of the Natural and the Unnatural: A Definition of the Gothic Romance." Diss. U of Pittsburgh, 1970. *DAI* 31 (1970): 2353A.

Thematic study of the Gothic novel considers Horace Walpole, William Beckford, Mary Shelley, and Ann Radcliffe, among others.

D11 Ronald, Margaret A. "Functions of Setting in the Novel: From Mrs. Radcliffe to Charles Dickens." Diss. Northwestern U, 1970. *DAI* 31 (1971): 5373A.

Examines development of setting in novels including *Udolpho, Jane Eyre,* and *Bleak House.* Published (unrevised) in 1980.

1971

D12 Durant, David Sedgwick, Jr. "Ann Radcliffe's Novels: Experiments in Setting." Diss. U of North Carolina at Chapel Hill, 1971. *DAI* 32 (1972): 5225A-5226A.

Studies the relationship between Radcliffe's style and her fictional strategy. Radcliffe's use of the sublime is pre-Romantic. Published (revised) in 1980.

D13 Heller, Lynne Epstein. "Ann Radcliffe's Gothic Landscape of Fiction and the Various Influences upon it." Diss. New York U, 1971. *DAI* 32 (1972): 5735A.

Traces Radcliffe's sources, including Burke, Shakespeare, Gray, Collins, Rosa, Poussin. Published (unrevised) in 1980.

D14 Price, Frederick Wallace. "The Concept of Character in the Eighteenth-Century Gothic Romance." Diss. Princeton U, 1971. *DAI* 32 (1972): 6388A-89A.

Includes discussion of Radcliffe's passive heroes.

D15 Reed, Ronald L. "The Function of Folklore in Selected English Gothic Novels." Diss. Texas Tech U, 1971. *DAI* 33 (1972): 284A.

Analyzes folk elements, especially superstitions that create fear, in *The Castle of Otranto, The Old English Baron, The Monk, Melmoth the Wanderer,* and *The Mysteries of Udolpho.*

1972

D16   Lea, Sydney L. W., Jr. "Gothic to Fantastic: Readings in Supernatural Fiction." Diss. Yale U, 1972. *DAI* 34 (1973): 323A.

Includes discussion of the explained supernatural in *The Italian*. Published (unrevised) in 1980.

D17   Platzner, Robert Leonard. "The Metaphyscial Novel in England: The Romantic Phase." Diss. U of Rochester, 1972. *DAI*
33 (1972): 2390A.

Studies *Udolpho, The Monk, Melmoth the Wanderer, Jane Eyre,
Wuthering Heights, Frankenstein, The Island of Dr. Moreau, Tess
of the d'Urbervilles,* and *Lord Jim* to find that they all subordinate mimesis to alienation and transcendence. Published
(unrevised) in 1980.

D18   Stoler, John Andrew. "Ann Radcliffe: The Novel of Suspense
and Terror." Diss. U of Arizona, 1972. *DAI* 32 (1972): 5203A.

Discusses Radcliffe's techniques for creating suspense and
terror in terms of characters, plot, and setting. Published
(unrevised) in 1980.

1973

D19   Garrett, John. "Gothic Strains and Bourgeois Sentiments in
the Novels of Mrs. Ann Radcliffe and her Imitators." Diss.
Dalhousie U, Halifax, N. S., 1973.

The predominance of bourgeois sentiments over the Gothic
in Radcliffe influenced a tame variety of contemporary Gothics. Published (unrevised) in 1980.

D20   Van Luchene, Stephen Robert. "Essays in Gothic Fiction:
From Horace Walpole to Mary Shelley." Diss. U of Notre
Dame, 1973. *DAI* 34 (1974): 4220A.

Includes comparison of *Udolpho* and *The Monk*. Published
(unrevised) in 1980.

1974

D21   Bassin, Henry Alan. "The Gothic Transformation: Develop-
ments in the British Gothic Romance, 1764-1887." Diss. Indiana U, 1974. *DAI* 35 (1975): 6700A.

Udolpho reconciles classical and romantic values.

D22 Zirker, Joan McTigue. "The Gothic Tradition in English Fiction, 1764-1824." Diss. Indiana U, 1974. *DAI* 35 (1974): 422A.

Considers Walpole and Radcliffe as observing Burke's dictates for sublimity.

1975

D23 Roberts, Bette. "The Gothic Romance: Its Appeal to Women Writers and Readers in Late Eighteenth-Century England." Diss. U of Massachusetts, 1975. *DAI* 36 (1976): 6119A.

Includes *Udolpho* in discussion of the ambivalent appeal of Gothic novels to women readers. Published (unrevised) in 1980.

D24 Sedgwick, Eve Kosofsky. "The Coherence of Gothic Conventions." Diss. Yale U, 1975. *DAI* 37 (1976): 301A.

A thematic and assimilative study of the Gothic that concentrates on Thomas De Quincey and on Charlotte and Emily Brontë. Briefly discusses *The Italian* in terms of imprisonment, dreams that duplicate subsequent reality, and "the Unspeakable," represented by the confessional. Later versions include the 1980 Arno edition with substantial revisions of chapter 1 and the 1986 Methuen edition, which contains her 1981 *PMLA* article.

D25 Sherman, Leona F. "Ann Radcliffe and the Gothic Romance: A Psychoanalytic Approach." Diss. SUNY at Buffalo, 1975. *DAI* 36 (1975): 1536A.

A psychoanalytic and feminist reading of *Udolpho*. Discusses Radcliffe's novels as "subversive, protest literature" in which the imagery of danger and repression expresses the anxieties of middle-class women, and the castle symbolizes "a hostile, internalized environment." Published (unrevised) in 1980.

D26 Stone, Joseph Liberty, Jr. "Ann Radcliffe." Diss. Harvard U, 1975.

Not available from University Microfilms International.

D27 Thomson, John. "The Novels of Ann Radcliffe." Diss. U of Otago, New Zealand, 1975.

Studies all of Radcliffe's novels, arguing that her landscape assumes the position of a personality.

D28   Weiss, Frederick Norman. "Satiric Elements in Early Gothic Novels." Diss. U of Pennsylvania, 1975. *DAI* 36 (1975): 2860A-61A.

Discusses satire in *Otranto, Vathek, Udolpho,* and *The Monk.* Published (unrevised) in 1980.

1976

D29   Madoff, Mark Samuel. "Ambivalent and Nostalgic Attitudes in Selected Gothic Novels." Diss. U of British Columbia, 1976. *DAI* 38 (1977): 284A.

Includes discussion of the ambivalent attitude of *Romance of the Forest, Udolpho,* and *The Italian,* among other Gothic novels.

D30   Poovey, Mary Louise. "The Novel as Imaginative Order." Diss. U of Virginia, 1976. *DAI* 37 (1977): 4374A.

Considers *Otranto* and *Udolpho* as representative of the early transition to subjectivity.

D31   Reno, Robert Princeton. "The Gothic Visions of Ann Radcliffe and Matthew G. Lewis." Diss. Michigan State U, 1976. *DAI* 37 (1977): 7767A.

Examines Radcliffe's novels and compares *Udolpho* and *The Italian* to *The Monk.* Published (unrevised) in 1980.

1977

D32   Adickes, Sandra Elaine. "The Social Quest: The Expanded Vision of Four Women Travelers in the Era of the French Revolution." Diss. New York U, 1977. *DAI* 38 (1978): 7308A.

Discusses the travels/travel writing of Mary Wollstonecraft, Helen Maria Williams, Ann Radcliffe, and Mary Berry. Published in 1991.

D33   Astle, Richard Sharp. "Structures of Ideology in the English Gothic Novel." Diss. U of California, San Diego, 1977. *DAI* 38 (1978): 5490A.

In *Udolpho* the tyranny of Emily's surrogate parents (her aunt and step-uncle) contradicts the parental approval of her real father, and the rationality of the explained supernatural contradicts the obscurity of Burkean sublimity.

D34 Bauska, Kathy Anderson. "The Feminine Dream of Happiness: A Study of the Woman's Search for Intelligent Love and Recognition in Selected English Novels from *Clarissa* to *Emma*." Diss. U of Washington, 1977. *DAI* 38 (1977): 1403A.

Udolpho provides a link between Richardson and Austen.

D35 Bowman, Barbara. "The Gothic Novel: A Structuralist Inquiry." Diss. U of Maryland, 1977. *DAI* 38 (1978): 4175A.

Structuralist approach to the early Gothic novel includes analyses of *Udolpho, Otranto, The Monk,* and *Melmoth the Wanderer*.

D36 Ehlers, Leigh Ann. "From Polarity to Perspective: The Development of Structure and Character in Gothic Fiction." Diss. U of Florida, 1977. *DAI* 39 (1978): 294A.

Considers Radcliffe's *The Italian* in examination of Walpole, Reeve, Lewis, Maturin, and Mary Shelley.

D37 Keeling, Thomas Harvey. "The Grotesque Vision: Structure and Aesthetics in the British Gothic Novel." Diss. U of California, Los Angeles, 1977. *DAI* 38 (1977): 2809A.

Includes an analysis of the grotesque in *The Italian*.

D38 Koenig, Linda Ruth. "Ann Radcliffe and Gothic Fiction." Diss. U of Iowa, 1977. *DAI* 39 (1978): 297A-98A.

Analyzes Radcliffe's development and improvement.

D39 Lewis, Paul. "Fearful Questions, Fearful Answers: The Intellectual Functions of Gothic Fiction." Diss. U of New Hampshire, 1977. *DAI* 38 (1977): 2791A-2792A.

Examines British and American Gothic writers. Analyzes how Walpole, Reeve, Radcliffe, and Lewis use the resolution of mystery for didactic ends.

D40 Reddin, Chitra Pershad. "Forms of Evil in the Gothic Novel." Diss. Dalhousie U, 1977.

Considers Radcliffe's villains, moral ambivalence, theme of deception by sense impressions, and portrayal of Nature as hostile. Published (unrevised) in 1980.

1978

D41   English, Sarah Warder. "The Hunger of Imagination: A Study of the Prose Style of Four Gothic Novels." Diss. U of North Carolina, 1978. *DAI* 39 (1979): 6773A-74A.

Argues that the prose style of *Otranto, The Old English Baron, Udolpho,* and *The Monk* is formal, artificial, and mechanical.

1980

D42   Jacobs, Maureen Sheehan. "Beyond the Castle: The Development of the Paradigmatic Female Story." Diss. American U, 1980. *DAI* 41 (1980): 679A-680A.

Interprets women's role of victim in Gothics written by women, focusing on female search for identity. Discusses *Udolpho* and goes on to consider Gothic revisionism in *Jane Eyre* and *Northanger Abbey.*

D43   Platt, Constance McCormick. "Patrimony as Power in Four Eighteenth-Century Women's Novels: Charlotte Lennox, *Henrietta* (1758); Fanny Burney, *Evelina* (1778); Charlotte Smith, *Emmeline* (1788); Ann Radcliffe, *The Mysteries of Udolpho* (1794)." Diss. U of Denver, 1980. *DAI* 41 (1981): 3595A.

A study of the relationship between fathers and daughters.

1981

D44   Ferguson, Mary Louise Dechert. "My Spectre around Me: The Reluctant Rebellion of the Gothic Novelists." Diss. Vanderbilt U, 1981. *DAI* 42 (1982): 4457A.

A response to the depravity of *The Monk, The Italian* actually shows that Lewis' ethos had become a part of the bourgeois English character.

D45   Peavoy, John Roger. "Artificial Terrors and Real Horrors: The Supernatural in Gothic Fiction." Diss. Brandeis U, 1981. *DAI* 42 (1981): 714A.

Discusses the supernatural in Radcliffe's novels, including *Gaston.*

D46   Valley, June Banks. "Characterization of the Gothic Heroine in Ann Radcliffe's Works." Diss. Howard U, 1981. *DAI* 43 (1982): 1984A.

Analyzes the development, representation as adolescents, and psychological ambiguity of Radcliffe's heroines.

D47   Weissman, Alan. "Thoughts in Things: Ann Radcliffe as a Psychological Novelist." Diss. City U of New York, 1981. *DAI* 42 (1982): 4013A.

Argues that Radcliffe helped pioneer the psychological novel.

1983

D48   Jennings, Richard Jerome. "La Fenêtre gothique: The Influence of Tragic Form on the Structure of the Gothic Novel." Diss. Ball State U, 1983. *DAI* 44 (1983): 760A.

Relates the Gothic novel (including *The Italian*) to classical tragedy.

1984

D49   Mathews, John Robert. "Ghostly Language: A Theory of Gothic Discourse." Diss. Cornell U, 1984. *DAI* 45 (1984): 529A.

Includes analysis of the psychological and rhetorical structure of Radcliffe's Gothic image.

D50   Nollen, Elizabeth Mahn. "The Gothic Experience: Female Imprisonment, Madness, and Escape in Selected Texts by Women Writers." Diss. Indiana U, 1984. *DAI* 46 (1986): 159A.

Analyzes *The Romance of the Forest* and *Udolpho* to argue that Radcliffe's Gothic begins a tradition of novels by women writers.

D51   Tamkin, Linda Ellen. "Heroines in Italy: Studies in the Novels of Ann Radcliffe, George Eliot, Henry James, E.M. Forster, and D.H. Lawrence." Diss. U of California, Los Angeles, 1984. *DAI* 45 (1985): 2536A.

Deals with the Italian journeys of heroines (including Emily St. Aubert) who experience powerful reactions to the landscape.

1985

D52   Bailey, Jutta M. "A Study of Women Characters in Selected Novels of Women Writers of the Romantic Period." Diss. U of Arkansas, 1985. *DAI* 46 (1986): 3024A.

Includes analysis of Emily in *Udolpho.*

D53   Johnson, Deborah Meem. "The Inner Epic Tradition in Nineteenth-Century Novels by Women." Diss. State U of New York
at Stony Brook, 1985. *DAI* 47 (1986): 898A.

Includes discussion of the inner epic in Radcliffe's works.

1986

D54   Carter, Margaret Louise. "'Fiend, Spectre, or Delusion?': Narrative Doubt and the Supernatural in Gothic Fiction." Diss.
U of California, Irvine, 1986. *DAI* 47 (1986): 908A.

A study of the supernatural in Gothic fiction of the eighteenth and nineteenth centuries, this dissertation includes a
consideration of Radcliffe's protagonists. Published (revised)
in 1987.

D55   Ede, W.R. "The Gentlewoman as Creative Artist in the Life
and Romances of Ann Radcliffe: 1764-1823." Diss. U of Wales,
1986.

D56   Grenier, Cecilia Marie. "Martyrs, Mystics and Madwomen:
Images of the Nun in Selected Fiction, 1780-1840." Diss. State
U of New York at Binghamton, 1986. *DAI* 47 (1986): 524A.

Discusses the nun in *Udolpho* and *The Italian.*

D57   Murphy, Ann Brian. "Persephone in the Underworld: The
Motherless Hero in Novels by Burney, Radcliffe, Austen,
Brontë, Eliot, and Woolf." Diss. U of Massachusetts, 1986.
DAI 47 (1987): 3436A.

Radcliffe's novels allow maternal energy to disrupt and rede-
fine.

D58   Pribek, Thomas Robert. "Utility and Invention in American
Gothic Literature." Diss. U of Wisconsin, 1986. *DAI* 47 (1987):
3429A.

Includes discussion of Walpole, Radcliffe, and Lewis.

1987

D59   Hagedorn, Jutta Angelika. "Der gotische Roman als sozialer
Roman des späten achtzehnten Jahrhunderts: Eine
vergleichende Studie englischer und deutscher gotischer und

sozialer Romane." Diss. U of Georgia, 1987. *DAI* 48 (1988): 2057A.

In German. Includes analysis of social themes in *Udolpho*.

D60 Tofanelli, John L. "The Gothic Confessional: Language and Subjectivity in the Gothic Novel, *Villette*, and *Bleak House*." Diss. Stanford U, 1987. *DAI* 48 (1988): 1780A.

Discusses the tyrannical Roman Catholic Church in *The Italian*.

1988

D61 David, Gail Pliam. "Diverse (In)Versions: Female Heroics in the Renaissance Pastoral Romance and in Women's Pastoral Fiction from Fanny Burney to George Eliot." Diss. U of California, Davis, 1988. *DAI* 50 (1989): 448A.

Analyzes female pattern in *Udolpho* as a reworking of pastoral inversion.

D62 Derry, Stephen Gerald. "Tradition, Imitation, and Innovation: Jane Austen and the Development of the Novel, 1740-1818." Diss. U of Durham, 1988. *DAI* 50 (1990): 3234A.

Discusses influence of Radcliffe (among others) on Austen.

D63 Heller, Wendy Tamar. "Wilkie Collins and the Female Gothic: A Study in the Politics of Genre and Literary Revision." Diss. Yale U, 1988. *DAI* 50 (1989): 1311A.

Begins study of Collins' revision of female Gothic tradition with a discussion of the Radcliffean Gothic. Published version, 1992.

D64 Lemmens, Cheryl Ann. "Dark Recesses of the Soul: Victimization in Selected British Fiction from *Clarissa* to *The Collector*." Diss. U of Toronto, 1988. *DAI* 53 (1992): 505A.

Investigates victimization theme in *Udolpho*.

1989

D65 Bohls, Elizabeth. "Aesthetics and Ideology in the Writings of Ann Radcliffe." Diss. Stanford U, 1989. *DAI* 50 (1990): 3959A.

Dismisses the usual categories applied to Radcliffe's novels (Gothic, sentimental) as inadequate. Instead, discusses

Radcliffe's works in terms of aesthetic disinterestedness and the ideology of femininity.

D66   Duncan, Ian Hamish. "Modern Romance: The Gothic, Scott, Dickens." Diss. Yale U, 1989. *DAI* 50 (1990): 3600A.

Discusses relationship between Scott and Radcliffe.

D67   Fitzgerald, Laurie Ann. "Multiple Genres in Five Late Eighteenth-Century Novels." Diss. U of Wisconsin, 1989. *DAI* 50 (1990): 2906A.

Analyzes the interrelationships of various genres in *The Italian.*

D68   Griesinger, Emily Ann. "Before and after *Jane Eyre:* The Female Gothic and some Modern Variations." Diss. Vanderbilt U, 1989. *DAI* 51 (1990): 511A-512A.

Studies literary revision by comparing five twentieth-century novels by women to *Udolpho* and to *Jane Eyre.*

D69   Lemberg-Welfonder, Marlis. "Ann Radcliffes Beitrag zur englischen Rousseau-Rezeption im Zeitalter der französischen Revolution." Diss. Ruprecht-Karls-Universität zu Heidelberg, 1989.

Studies the influence of Rousseau on Radcliffe.

D70   McCormick, Marjorie Jean. "Mothers in the English Novel: From Stereotype to Archetype." Diss. Vanderbilt U, 1989. *DAI* 50 (1989): 1667A.

Includes brief discussion of mothers in Radcliffe's novels.

D71   Mengay, Donald Henry, Jr. "Monsters and Menaces: A Study in the Dynamics of Being Other in the Gothic Novel." Diss. New York U, 1989. *DAI* 50 (1990): 2889A.

A study of otherness in *Udolpho, Frankenstein, Melmoth the Wanderer,* and *Teleny.*

D72   Wolstenholme, Susan Carol. "Gothic Visions and Writing Women: Radcliffe, Shelley, Stowe, Eliot." Diss. Cornell U, 1989. *DAI* 50 (1990): 2914A.

Radcliffe chapter discusses *The Italian* in terms of the male "gaze." Revised and expanded version published in 1993.

1990

D73 Bernstein, Stephen David. "Fugitive Genre: Gothicism, Ideology, and Intertextuality." Diss. U of Wisconsin, 1990. *DAI* 51 (1991): 3078A-79A.

Includes an exploration of gothic ideology in the works of Walpole, Radcliffe, Lewis, Maturin.

D74 Bowen, Kevin Joseph. "The Gothic Novel in England: Studies in a Literary Mode." Diss. State U of New York, Buffalo, 1990. *DAI* 52 (1991): 166A.

Includes analysis of the changing reception of Radcliffe's works.

1991

D75 Greenfield, Susan Celia. "Novel Daughters: The Family Romance from Frances Burney to Jane Austen." Diss. U of Pennsylvania, 1991. *DAI* 52 (1991): 926A.

Discusses Radcliffe's use of the maternal myth. Argues that the mother-daughter love in *The Italian* has homoerotic overtones.

D76 O'Dea, Gregory Sean. "The Temporal Sublime: Time and History in the British Gothic Novel." Diss. U of North Carolina at Chapel Hill, 1991. *DAI* 52 (1992): 2563A.

Discusses Radcliffe's use of the sublime.

1992

D77 Moore, Alice Frances. "'Dark, Irate, and Piercing': Male Heroes of Female-Authored Gothic Novels." Diss. U of Massachusetts, 1992. *DAI* 53 (1992): 1927A.

Investigates sadomasochism in Radcliffe's works.

1993

D78 Byam, Paige Beresford. "Mysteries in Narrative: Female Figures, Fear, and the Disruption of Telos." Diss. U of Wisconsin, 1993. *DAI* 54 (1994): 2565A.

Analyzes Emily as a mystery figure in *Udolpho*.

D79 Herrera, C. Andrea O'Reilly. "Nuns and Lovers: Tracing the Development of Idyllic Conventual Writing." Diss. U of Delaware, 1993. *DAI* 54 (1994): 2588A.

Deals with the imaginary convent and nun in Radcliffe's works.

D80   Jackson, Jessamyn. "Women of Feeling: Female Sensibility in Eighteenth-Century English Novels and Conduct Literature." Diss. Yale U, 1993. *DAI* 54 (1994): 3040A.

Udolpho "deconstructs the negative stereotypes of sensibility that it ostensibly endorses."

D81   Wenner, Barbara Ann Britton. "Prospect and Refuge: Heroines in Nineteenth-Century Novelistic Landscape." Diss. U of Cincinnati, 1993. *DAI* 54 (1993): 2160A.

In *Udolpho* Emily is caught between two landscapes that are conflicting.

D82   Woodard, Anne. "Gender Role Reversal in Gothic and Romantic Fiction: 1790-1830 (English and French)." Diss. Catholic U of America, 1993. *DAI* 53 (1993): 3898A.

Otranto, Udolpho, and *Northanger Abbey* reveal the insufficiency of traditional gender roles.

9

BIBLIOGRAPHIES (B)

1941

B1   Summers, Montague. *A Gothic Bibliography*. 1941. NY: Russell and Russell, 1964.

Pioneering reference guide lists Radcliffe's works, as well as adaptations and spurious attributions.

1969

B2   Watson, George. *The New Cambridge Bibliography of English Literature*. Cambridge: Cambridge UP, 1969. 3:758-60.

Sketchy bibliography of Radcliffe's works.

1973

B3   Forstner, L.J. and A.C. Elkins, Jr., eds. *The Romantic Movement Bibliography: 1936-1970*. Ann Arbor: The Pierian Press, 1973.

Scattered entries on Radcliffe.

B4   Frank, Frederick S. "The Gothic Novel: A Checklist of Modern Criticism." *Bulletin of Bibliography and Magazine Notes* 30 (1973): 45-54.

Bibliography of Gothic novels includes Radcliffe. Incorporated into Frank's later bibliographies.

1974

B5   Lévy, Maurice. "English Gothic and the French Imagination:
A Calendar of Translations, 1767-1828." In Thompson, Gary
Richard, ed. *The Gothic Imagination: Essays in Dark Romanti-
cism.* Pullman: Washington State UP, 1974. 150-76.

Bibliography of French translations of English Gothic novels
includes Radcliffe.

1975

B6   Frank, Frederick S. "A Bibliography of Writings about Ann
Radcliffe." *Extrapolation* 17 (1975): 54-62.

Useful if incomplete annotated bibliography of 52 secondary
sources from 1900 to 1971. For expanded versions, see Frank's
later bibliographies (B13 and B22).

B7   McNutt, Dan. *The Eighteenth-Century Gothic Novel.* NY and London: Garland, 1975.

Annotated bibliographies of the Gothic and of Walpole,
Reeve, Smith, Radcliffe, Lewis, and Beckford. Through 1975
with omissions.

1976

B8   Dunn, Richard J., ed. *The English Novel: Twentieth Century
Criticism.* Chicago: The Swallow Press, 1976. 1: 121-22.

Brief bibliography.

1977

B9   Backscheider, Paula, Felicity Nussbaum, and Philip B. Anderson. *An Annotated Bibliography of Twentieth-Century Critical Studies of Women and Literature, 1660-1800.* NY and London: Garland, 1977.

Brief annotated bibliography.

1978

B10   Beasley, Jerry C. *English Fiction, 1660-1800: A Guide to Information Sources.* Detroit: Gale Research Company, 1978. 193-98.

Brief lists of works, editions, biographies, and critical studies.

1981

B11 Frank, Frederick S. "The Gothic Romance 1762-1820." *Horror Literature: A Core Collection and Reference Guide.* Ed. Marshall B. Tymm. NY: R.R. Bowker, 1981. 3-175.

Overview that considers Radcliffe's novels to have "determined the course of the Gothic movement during its mature phase" (22). Annotated primary bibliography follows.

1983

B12 Graham, John. *Novels in English: The Eighteenth- and Nineteenth-Century Holdings at Schloss Corvey, Höxter, Germany.* NY and Berne: Peter Lang, 1983.

This bibliographical record of the Corvey library holdings includes editions of Radcliffe.

1984

B13 Frank, Frederick S. *Guide to the Gothic.* Metuchen, NJ and London: Scarecrow Press, 1984.

Guide to Gothic writers by nationality. Radcliffe section consists of annotated version of 1988 bibliography with several more entries. See also Frank's 1975 bibliography (B6).

B14 Spector, Robert Donald. *The English Gothic: A Bibliographic Guide to Writers from Horace Walpole to Mary Shelley.* Westport, Connecticut and London: Greenwood Press, 1984. 122-52.

Includes bibliographic essay on Radcliffe.

B15 Rev. by Margaret Carter in *Eighteenth-Century Studies* 21 (1988): 364-67.

1985

B16 Hahn, H. George and Carl Behm III. *The Eighteenth-Century British Novel and its Background: An Annotated Bibliography and Guide to Topics.* Metuchen, NJ and London: Scarecrow Press, 1985.

Brief annotated bibliography.

1986

B17   Galli Mastrodonato, Paola. "Romans gothiques anglais et
traductions françaises: L'Année 1797 et la migration de
récits." *Neohelicon* 13 (1986): 287-320.

In French. Article on French translations of English Gothic
novels includes Radcliffe.

B18   Lund, Roger D. "The Modern Reader and the 'Truly Femi-
nine Novel,' 1660-1815: A Critical Reading List." *Fetter'd or
Free? British Women Novelists, 1670-1815.* Ed. Mary Anne
Schofield and Cecilia Macheski. Athens, Ohio and London:
Ohio UP, 1986. 398-425.

Includes brief reflection on critical studies of Radcliffe.

1987

B19   Frank, Frederick S. *The First Gothics: A Critical Guide to the
English Gothic Novel.* NY and London: Garland, 1987.

Essential bibliography of 500 Gothics published from 1762 to
1832 includes Radcliffe. Provides brief "Critical Synopsis" of
each. In many instances goes beyond Summers.

B20   Rev. by Devendra P. Varma in *Eighteenth-Century Fiction* 1 (1989): 165-70.

1988

B21   Fisher, Benjamin Franklin, IV. *The Gothic's Gothic: Study Aids
to the Tradition of the Tale of Terror.* NY and London: Garland,
1988. 16-27.

Includes brief annotated bibliography of Radcliffe criticism
from 1797 to 1976. Many omissions.

B22   Frank, Frederick S. *Gothic Fiction: A Master List of Twentieth-
Century Criticism and Research.* Westport, CT: Meckler, 1988.
41-49.

Includes checklist of Gothic writers by nationality. Repeats
much of Frank's 1984 bibliography (B13) without annota-
tion. See also Frank's 1975 bibliography (B6).

1991

B23 Rogers, Deborah D. "Ann Radcliffe in the 1980s: An Annotated Bibliography of Criticism." *Extrapolation* 32 (1991): 343-
49.

Annotated bibliography demonstrates that the decade saw
renewed interest in Radcliffe.

1992

B24 Smith, Margaret M. and Alexander Lindsay, eds. Vol. 3, Pt. 3
of *Index of English Literary Manuscripts.* NY: Mansell, 1992.

Describes the few extant Radcliffe manuscripts.

APPENDIX I:
ADAPTATIONS AND ABRIDGMENTS

ADAPTATIONS

THE CASTLES OF ATHLIN AND DUNBAYNE

ENGLISH

1806

Manners, George. *Edgar; or Caledonian Feuds.* London: Tipper and Richards, 1806.

1809

Cross, J.D. *Halloween* (1809).

A SICILIAN ROMANCE

ENGLISH

1794

Siddons, Henry. *The Sicilian Romance; or, the Apparition of the Cliffs.* London: Barker, 1794.

Operatic adaptation.

Praised for its "variety, and the succesion of serious and

comic scenes" in *European Magazine and London Review* 25 (1794): 467.

Criticized as a "very slight piece . . . with a very full dose of ghosts, plots, dungeons, iron doors, and all the paraphernalia of the tragic muse" in *Critical Review* 13 (1795): 338.

FRENCH

1798

Julia, ou les souterrains de Mazzini. Produced at the théâtre des Jeunes-Artistes November, 1798.

THE ROMANCE OF THE FOREST

ENGLISH

1794

Boaden, James. *Fontainville Forest.* London: Printed for Hookham and Carpenter, 1794.

Theatrical adaptation deviates from the novel by eliminating the character of Theodore. Condensed version, 1796.

Fair review in *British Critic* 4 (1794): 186-87.

Critical Review 11 (1794): 402-406 patronizingly praises *Romance of the Forest* for following the rules of the epic "though the fair authoress knew not, probably, of their existence . . ." (402-403). *Fontainville* fails in this respect, as well as in deviating from the novel's depiction of La Motte.

Positive review consisting mostly of plot summary and quotations in *English Review* 23 (1794): 455-58.

First performance praised in *European Magazine and London Review* 25 (1794): 308-10, where the play is summarized.

Boaden, himself, discusses his play in his *Memoirs of the Life of John Philip Kemble Esq. Including a History of the Stage from the Time of Garrick to the Present Period.* London: Printed for Longman, Hurst, Rees, Orme, Brown, and Green, 1825. 2: 96-100 and 116-119. [Boaden's biography of Kemble is reviewed negatively in *Westminster Review* 3 (1825): 487-99.]

1807

Dunlap, William. *Fontainville Abbey*. NY: David Longworth, 1807. Rptd. in *Four Plays*. Delmar, NY: Scholars' Facsimiles, 1976.

THE MYSTERIES OF UDOLPHO

ENGLISH

1803

Dunlap, William. *Ribbemont*. NY: David Longworth, 1803. Rptd. in *Four Plays*. Delmar, NY: Scholars' Facsimiles, 1976.

1808

Weston, Ferdinand Fullerton. *The Castle of Udolpho, A Dramatic Opera*. In *The Dramatic Apellant* (1808).

FRENCH

1798

Duval, Alexandre. *Montoni, ou le Château d'Udolphe*. Produced at the Théâtre de la Cité, 29 July, 1798.

Lamartelière, *Le Testament, ou les Mystères d'Udolphe*. Produced at the Théâtre Louvois, 1798.

1799

Hoffman, F. and Dalagrac. *Léon, ou le Château de Montenéro*. Produced at the théâtre de la rue Favant, 1799.

Réné-Charles Guilbert de Pixérécourt. *Le Château des Apennins, ou le Fantôme vivant*. Produced at the Ambigu-Comique, 9 December 1799.

Translated into English by John Baylis as *The Mysteries of Udolpho; or The Phantom of the Castle*, 1804.

A SICILIAN ROMANCE AND *THE MYSTERIES OF UDOLPHO*

ENGLISH

1795

Andrews, Miles Peter. *The Mysteries of the Castle.* London: Printed by W. Woodfall for T.N. Longman, 1795.

> *Critical Review* 14 (1795): 101 finds "The story is partly taken from Mrs. Radcliffe's excellent romance; but we fear that lady will not feel herself flattered by the relationship."

> Panned as an "absurd mixture of tragedy, comedy, farce, opera, and pantomime" in *European Magazine and London Review* 27 (1795): 124.

> Positive review in *Universal Magazine* 96 (1795): 136-37.

1807

White, J.B. *The Mysteries of the Castle.* Charleston, SC: J. Hoff, 1807.

> American version of Andrews' work of the same title with few changes.

THE ITALIAN

ENGLISH

1797

Boaden, James. *The Italian Monk.* London: G. G. and J. Robinson, 1797.

> Theatrical adaptation.

> Positive review in *Monthly Magazine* 4 [Supplement] (1797): 517. Approves of the play's reclamation of Schedoni because "the scene of this monk's death, in the original, if success-fully copied, might have been too tragical for the stage."

> Mixed rev. in *Monthly Mirror* 4 (1797): 100-103.

> Negative rev. in *Monthly Review* 24 (1797): 464 finds the play "displays exactly genius enough in the common scenes to

disappoint the reader in those which require a prominence of pathos. . . ."

Smith, Elihu Hubbard. Entry dated 10 December 1797. *The Diary of Elihu Hubbard Smith.* Ed. James E. Cronin. Philadelphia: American Philosophical Society, 1973. 401. Smith notes that he read *The Italian Monk* and remarks, "This play is poor enough but is very likely to please on the stage."

Boaden mentioned in passing in *Monthly Magazine* 7 (1799): 538 as having dramatized *The Italian* "with some little success."

Boaden, himself, discusses his play in his *Memoirs of the Life of John Philip Kemble Esq. Including a History of the Stage from the Time of Garrick to the Present Period.* London: Printed for Longman, Hurst, Rees, Orme, Brown, and Green, 1825. 2: 201-202. [Boaden's biography of Kemble is reviewed negatively in *Westminster Review* 3 (April 1825): 487-99.]

1805

The False Penitent; or, The Monk of Palluzi (1805).

FRENCH

1798

Pujos and Dabaytua. *Eléonore de Rosalba, ou les Ruines de Paluzzi.* Produced at the théâtre de la Cité, 5 June, 1798.

GASTON DE BLONDEVILLE

ENGLISH

Mitford, Mary Russell. *Gaston de Blondeville* (an unacted play) in *The Dramatic Works of Mary Russell Mitford.* London: Hurst and Blackett, 1854.

ABRIDGEMENTS

Many unauthorized chapbooks abridged Radcliffe's works. These include, for example:

A SICILIAN ROMANCE

The Southern Tower. London: T. Hurst, 1802.

Plagiarized abridgement alters Radcliffe's names.

THE MYSTERIES OF UDOLPHO

Chapbook of *Udolpho.* London: W. Mason, [17—?]

The Veiled Picture; or, The Mysteries of Gorgono, the Apennine Castle of Signor Androssi. A Romance of the Sixteenth Century. London: Thomas Tegg [1802].

Chapbook abridgement.

THE ITALIAN

The Midnight Assassin. Marvellous Magazine and Compendium of Prodigies 1 (May, 1802): unnumbered.

Pirated abridgement.

The Black Convent. London: Minerva Press for A.K. Newman, 1819.

Abridgement alters names and locale.

APPENDIX II:
PARODIES AND IMITATIONS

PARODIES

1797

[Beckford, William.] *Azemia*. London: S. Low, 1797.

> Rev. in *Monthly Mirror* 4 (1797): 95-97 finds that *Azemia* satirizes Radcliffe, Burney, and Piozzi, among others. (See Piozzi, 1804.)

1798

Patrick, F.C. *More Ghosts!* London: Minerva Press, 1798.

1799

Charlton, Mary. *Rosella, or Modern Occurrences*. London: Minerva Press for Lane, Newman, 1799.

1813

Barrett, Eaton Stannard. *The Heroine*. London: Henry Colburn, 1813.

> Throughout, scattered allusions to Radcliffe, whose works (especially *Udolpho*) influenced Cherry Wilkinson. (See, for example, 1: viii, 10, 19, 24; 2: 35, 217; 3: 1, 75, 114.)

1817

Austen, *Northanger Abbey*. London: John Murray. Published posthumously with *Persuasion* in Dec., 1817 (1818 on the title page).

> Parodies, alludes to, and is influenced by Radcliffe throughout.

IMITATIONS/FORGERIES/PLAGIARISMS

1792

The Castle of St. Vallery. London: G. and J. Robinson, 1792.

1793

Ashton Priory. London: Law, 1793

[Roche, Regina Maria.] *The Maid of the Hamlet*. London: Long, 1793.

1794

Kelly, Isabella. *Madeline; or, The Castle of Montgomery*. London: Minerva Press, 1794.

1795

The Abbey of St. Asaph (1795?)

> Rev. in *Critical Review* 14 (1795): 349 as a "humble imitation" of Radcliffe.

I.H. *The Phantoms of the Cloister*. London: Minerva Press for William Lane, 1795.

Kelly, Isabella. *The Abbey of Saint Asaph*. London: Minerva Press, 1795.

MacKenzie, Anna Maria. *Mysteries Elucidated*. London: Minerva Press for William Lane, 1795.

Meeke, Mary. *The Abbey of Clugny*. London: Minerva Press for William Lane, 1795.

Palmer, John, Jr. *The Haunted Cavern*. London: Crosby, 1795.

> Rev. in *English Review* 26 (1795): 468-73 claims this work was influenced by *Romance of the Forest* (468). Negative review provides evidence that the public was tiring of the Gothic:

In truth, we are almost weary of Gothic castles, mouldering turrets, and 'cloud inveloped battlements'—The tale of shrieking spectres, and bloody murders, has been repeated till it palls upon the sense. It requires the genius of a Radcliffe to harrow up our souls with these visionary terrors, and speak of ghosts that rise 'with twenty mortal murders on their crowns.'

1796

Austenburn Castle. London: Minerva Press for William Lane, 1796; Dublin: P. Wogan, P. Byrne, J. Rice, J. Boyce, and W. Porter, 1796.

Rev. in *Critical Review* 16 (1796): 222 categorizes this work as an imitation of Radcliffe. Notes the profusion of imitations: "Since Mrs. Radcliffe's justly admired and successful romances, the press has teemed with stories of haunted castles and visionary terrors; the incidents of which are so little diversified, that criticism is at a loss to vary its remarks."

Helme, Elizabeth. *The Farmer of Inglewood Forest.* London: Minerva Press for William Lane, 1796.

Kelly, Isabella. *The Ruins of Avondale Priory.* London: Minerva Press, 1796.

Robinson, Mary. *Hubert de Sevrac.* London: Hookham and Carpenter, 1796.

Rev. in *Critical Review* 23 (1798): 472 declares this novel to be an imitation of Radcliffe.

Roche, Regina Maria. *The Children of the Abbey.* London: Minerva Press for William Lane, 1796.

The Wanderer of the Alps: or, Alphonso (1796).

Rev. in *Critical Review* 2nd ser. 20 (1797): 352-353.

Charges the novel with imitating *Udolpho* in almost everything except the character of Osmond, where "the author suspends our disgust at the hackneyed and borrowed machinery of *haunted castles, skeletons, banditti,* &c." (353)

1797

Moore, George. *Grasville Abbey: A Romance*. Serialized in *Lady's Maga-zine* 24-28 (March 1793-August 1797); G.G. & J. Robinson, 1797.

Selden, Catherine. *The Count de Santerre*. London: C. Dilly, 1797.

1798

The Animated Skeleton. London: Minerva Press for William Lane, 1798.

Lansdell, Sarah. *The Tower*. Printed for the Authoress by Harry Smith, 1798.

MacKenzie, Anna Maria. *Dusseldorf: or the Fratricide*. London: Minerva Press for William Lane, 1798.

> Rev. in *Critical Review* ns 24 (October 1798): 236 refers to this novel as an imitation of Radcliffe.

Meeke, Mary. *The Sicilian*. London: Crosby and Letterman, 1798.

Mort Castle. London: J. Wallis, 1798.

Roche, Regina Maria. *Clermont*. London: Minerva Press for William Lane, 1798.

> Rev. in *Critical Review* 26 (1798): 356. "This tale reminds us, without any great pleasure, of Mrs. Radcliffe's romances."

Sicklemore, Richard. *Edgar, or the Phantom of the Castle*. London: Minerva Press for William Lane, 1798.

> Rev. in *Monthly Mirror* 6 (1798): 161 finds the novel a good imitation of Radcliffe, allowing that the author imitates "more successfully than the generality of his brother-writers, the manner of a lady so deservedly popular as Mrs. Radcliffe."

Sleath, Eleanor. *The Orphan of the Rhine*. London: Minerva Press, 1798.

> Rev. of *The Orphan of the Rhine. Critical Review* 27 (1799): 356. A "servile" imitation of Radcliffe.

Young, Mary Julia. *Rose-Mount Castle*. London: Minerva Press for William Lane, 1798.

1799

The Castles of Montreuil and Barre. London: S. Fisher, 1799.

Curties, T.J. Horsley. *Ethelwina.* London: Minerva Press for William Lane, 1799.

Proby, William Charles. *The Mysterious Seal.* London: Westley, 1799.

> Rev. in *Monthly Review* 30 (1799): 471 claims this novel copies scenes from *Udolpho.*

Thomas, Francis Tracy. *Monk-Wood Priory.* London: Longman and Rees, 1799.

Young, Mary Julia. *The East Indian.* London: Earle and Hemet, 1799.

1800

Elson, Jane. *Romance of the Castle.* London: Minerva Press for William Lane, 1800.

The Mysterious Penitent. London: Crosby and Letterman, 1800.

Proby, William Charles. *The Spirit of the Castle.* London: J.W. Myers for Crosby and Letterman, 1800.

The Spectre Mother. London: Dean and Munday, 1800.

1801

Curties, T.J. Horsley. *Ancient Records.* London: Minerva Press for William Lane, 1801.

Frere, Benjamin. *The Man of Fortitude; or, Schedoni in England.* 3 vols. London: Wallis, 1801.

> Positive rev. in *British Critic* 17 (1801): 435. Chief objection is financial: "One common fault of novels is to be observed of this; the design on the reader's pocket is immediately obvious; a story is divided into three volumes, for which twelve shillings is demanded, when, in fact, it ought to be comprized in one volume, at less than half the price."

Helme, Elizabeth. *St. Margaret's Cave.* London: Earle and Hemet, 1801.

Isaacs, Mrs. Supposed author. *Ariel.* London: Minerva Press for William Lane, 1801.

1802

Harvey, Jane. *Minerva Castle*. London: Minerva Press for Lane and Newman, 1802.

Harvey, Jane. *Warkfield Castle*. London: Minerva Press for Lane and Newman, 1802.

1803

Bromley, Elizabeth Nugent. *The Cave of Cosenza*. London: W. Calvert for G. and J. Robinson, 1803.

The Ghost of Harcourt. Minerva Press for Lane, Newman, 1803.

1804

Crookenden, Isaac. *The Story of Morella de Alto*. London: S. Fisher, 1804.

Drake, Nathan. "The Abbey of Clunedale." *Literary Hours*. London: T. Cadell and W. Davies, 1804.

Horatio and Camilla. London: Ann Lemoine, 1804.

Valombrosa. London: Minerva Press for Lane, Newman, 1804.

> Rev. in *Critical Review* 43 (1805): 329 claims this novel is to be ranked among the innumberable imitations of *Udolpho* "with which the press has groaned. . . ." Criticizes the author for having "the slightest ambition to imitate that delicacy which is one of the many beauties so profusely scattered over the writings of Mrs. Radcliffe."

1805

The Castle of Santa Fe. London: Minerva Press for Lane, Newman, 1805.

Isaacs, Mrs. *Glenmore Abbey*. London: Minerva Press for Lane, Newman, 1805.

Morley, G.T. *Deeds of Darkness*. London: Tipper and Richards, 1805.

Picard, Mary. *The Castle of Roviego*. London: J. Barfield for J. Booth, 1805.

Selden, Catherine. *Villa Nova*. London: Connor, Cork for Lane, Newman, 1805.

1806

Crookenden, Isaac. *Fatal Secrets.* London: J. Lee, 1806.

Dellingborough Castle. London: Minerva Press for Lane, Newman, 1806.

Hamilton, Ann Mary. *The Forest of Saint Bernardo.* London: J.F. Hughes, 1806.

Hamilton, Liss. *The Forest of Montalbano.* 1806.

Harvey, Jane. *The Castle of Tynemouth.* London: Vernor and Hood, 1806.

Manners, Mrs. *Castle Nouvier.* London: B. Crosby, 1806.

1807

Curties, T.J. Horsley. *The Monk of Udolpho.* London: D.N. Shury for J.F. Hughes, 1807.

Stuart, Augusta Amelia. *Ludovico's Tale; or, The Black Banner of Castle Douglas.* 1807.

1808

Crookenden, Isaac. *Horrible Revenge.* London: R. Harrild, 1808.

Ratcliffe, Eliza. *The Mysterious Baron.* London: Minerva Press for Lane, Newman, 1808.

1809

The Convent of St. Ursula. London: John Arliss, 1809.

Smith, Catherine. *The Castle of Aragon.* London: Henry Colburn, 1809.

Wilkinson, Sarah. *The Mysterious Novice.* London: Arliss, 1809.

1810

Cowley, Hannah Parkhouse. *The Italian Marauders.* London: J. Dean for George Hughes, 1810.

Cuthbertson, C. *The Forest of Montalbano.* London: George Robinson, 1810.

> Trans. as *Angelina, oder die Abentheuer im Walde von Montalbano.* Brunswick: 1828. Trans. into French in 1813. Both translations have been spuriously attributed to Radcliffe.

Harwood, C. *The Castle of Vivaldi.* London: Minerva Press for A.K. Newman, 1810.

Houghton, Mary. *The Mysteries of the Forest.* London: Minerva Press for A.K. Newman, 1810.

Lambe, George. *The Mysteries of Ferney Castle.* London: B. Clarke for Henry Colburn, 1810.

1811

C. *The Banditti of the Forest.* Serialized in 8 parts in *Lady's Monthly Museum, or Polite Repository of Amusement and Instruction.* 9-10 (July, 1811-February, 1812): 248-67, 311-36, 415-34, 563-88, 640-661, 697-722, 31-50, 102-42.

Crookenden, Isaac. *The Italian Banditti.* London: R. Harrild, 1811.

Rosalie. London: Longman, Hurst, Rees, and Orme, 1811.

> Rev. in *Monthly Review* 67 (1812): 320-21 claims that Radcliffe's heroines provide the models for this work.

Sleath, Eleanor. *Pyrenean Banditti.* London: Minerva Press for A.K. Newman, 1811.

1812

Curtis, Julia Ann Kemble. *Sicilian Mysteries.* London: Henry Colburn, 1812.

Doherty, Ann. *The Castles of Wolfnorth and Monteagle.* London: Hookham, 1812.

Stanhope, Louisa Sidney. *The Confessional of Valombre.* London: Minerva Press for A.K. Newman, 1812.

1813

The Chapel of St. Benedict. Belle Assemblee, or Bell's Court and Fashionable Magazine 8-10 (September, 1813-July, 1814). Serialized in 11 parts.

1814

Green, Sarah. *The Cathusian Friar.* London: Sherwood, Neely, and Jones; C. Chapple, 1814.

Haynes, D.F. *Pierre and Adeline.* London: B. Crosby, 1814.

Pilkington, Mary. *The Novice.* London: Minerva Press for A.K. Newman, 1814.

Scott, Honoria. *The Castle of Strathmay.* London: Tegg, 1814.

1815

Curtis, Julia Ann Kemble. *The Secret Avengers.* Minerva Press for A.K. Newman, 1815.

1816

Rouvière, Henrietta. *Craig Melrose Abbey.* London: Chapple, 1816.

1817

Alexena. London: Minerva Press for A.K. Newman, 1817.

1818

The Bandit Chief. London: Minerva Press for A.K. Newman, 1818.

Madame la Comtesse de Nardouet. *Barbarinski.* Paris: 1818. French imitation.

1819

Brown, Elizabeth Cullen. *The Sisters of St. Gothard.* London: Minerva Press for A.K. Newman, 1819.

The Castle of Villa-Flora. London: Minerva Press for A.K. Newman, 1819.

1820

Hales, J.M.H. *The Astrologer.* London: William Fearman, 1820.

Layton, Mrs. Frederick. *Hulme Abbey.* London: William Fearman, 1820.

1821

Haynes, C.D. *Eleanor.* London: A.K. Newman, 1821.

1824

Bolen, C.A. *Le Panache rouge.* Paris: 1824. French imitation.

1826

Bolen, C.A. *The Mysterious Monk.* London: A.K. Newman, 1826.

APPENDIX III:
SPURIOUS ATTRIBUTIONS

1798

L'Abbaye de Grasville. Paris: 1798.

>French translation by Ducas of George Moore's *Grasville Abbey* spuriously attributed to Radcliffe.

Le paure di Matilde; o, La Badia di Grasvilla. Milan: Fratelli Ferrario [n.d.].

>Translation of George Moore's *Grasville Abbey* spuriously attributed to Radcliffe.

1798-99

Le Tombeau. Paris: Barba & André, [1798-99]. Another edn. published in 1812.

>Supposedly Radcliffe's posthumous work! The "translators," H. Chaussier and Bizet, are the actual authors.

1798-1812

Baillie, Joanna. *Plays on the Passions* (1798-1812).

>Attributed by some to Radcliffe.

1799

Radcliffe, Mary Ann. *The Female Advocate* (1799).

L'Avocat des femmes was also mistakenly attributed to Ann Radcliffe.

1801

Die Einsiedlerin am Vesuv. Trans. Konrad Adolf Hartleben (1801).

1803

Les Visions du Château des Pyrénées (1803).

> Supposedly trans. of Radcliffe, but actually an original work by Count Garnier and Mdlle. Zimmermann. Dutch version published in 1820. German translation published in 1818.

1809

Radcliffe, Mary Ann. *Manfroné* (1809). London: Hughes, 1809.

> Frequently attributed to Ann Radcliffe.

1810

Le Couvent de Sainte Catherine. Paris: 1810.

> Supposedly translated—but actually written—by Baroness Caroline d'Aufdiener.

1813

La Forêt de Montalbano. Paris: 1813.

> Translation of Catherine Cuthbertson's *Forest of Montalbano* (1810) or possibly of Liss Hamilton's *Forest of Montalbano* (1806).

1815

Hermite de la Tombe Mystérieuse.

> Supposedly translated—but actually written by the Baron de la Mothe-Langon [Mothe-Houdancourt]. Translated into German, 1817.

1817

Kesteren, J.C. van. *De Albigenzen of de Kluizenaar in het bosch van Caillavel.* Amsterdam: 1817.

1818

Die Erscheinungen im Schlosse der Pyrenäen (1818).

1819

Les Mystères de la Tour de Saint-Jean. Paris: Chez Corbet, 1819.

> Spuriously attributed to Radcliffe or to Matthew Gregory Lewis. Supposedly translated—but may have actually been written—by the Baron de la Mothe-Langon [Mothe-Houdancourt].

1824

Die Priorin. Brunswick: 1824.

> Actually a translation of W.H. Ireland's *The Abbess* (1799).

1828

Angelina oder die Abentheuer im Walde von Montalbano. Brunswick: 1828.

> A translation of Catherine Cuthbertson's *Forest of Montalbano* (1810).

1829

Das schwarze Schloss, oder der Sturm der Leidenschaften. Brunswick: 1829.

> Translation of G.D. Hernon's *Louisa* (1805).

Der Thurm von Aosta, oder Grossmuth im Tode. Brunswick: 1829.

1830

Rose d'Altenberg. Trans. M. Henri Duval. Paris: 1830.

> Attributed to Radcliffe. [Madame Brayer de Saint-Léon's *Alexina* (1813) was published by Campbell as her own work, *The Midnight Wanderer*, which Duval re-translated as Radcliffe's.]

Die Todeswette. Trans. Gustav Seller. Pesth: 1830.

1835

Brayer de Saint-Léon, Louise Marguerite Jeanne Madeleine. *L'Ombre de la Marquise de Crequy aux lecteurs des souvenirs*. Paris: Roret, 1835.

1871

Gli assassini di Ercolano. Milan: 1871.

18–?

Ellena: A Romance. Cincinnati: U.P. James, [18 ?].

The Chamber Mystery. Glasgow: Cameron and Ferguson, [18 ?].

MISCELLANEOUS

I fantasmi del castello [di] Anna Radcliffe. Rome: Capriotti, [1944].

INDEX

Page numbers refer to pages in the biography and appendices. Alphanumeric codes refer to the following sections:

P Primary Bibliography: Editions and Translations (pp. 23-34)
E Early Reviews and Notices, 1789-1826 (pp. 35-62)
C Criticism, 1827-1899 (pp. 63-80)
T Twentieth-Century Criticism, Part I: 1900-1949 (pp. 81-98)
TC Twentieth-Century Criticism, Part II: 1950-Present (pp. 99-147)
F Full-length Works (pp. 149-53)
D Dissertations (pp. 155-68)
B Bibliographies (pp. 169-73)

About the Author

DEBORAH D. ROGERS is Professor of English at the University of Maine. Her books include *Bookseller as Rogue: John Almon and the Politics of Eighteenth-Century Publishing* (1986), *The Critical Response to Ann Radcliffe* (Greenwood, 1994), and *Two Gothic Classics by Women* (1995). Her articles have appeared in publications such as *Eighteenth-Century Studies, Eighteenth-Century Fiction, Clio, The Journal of American Studies,* and *The New York Times.*

ISBN 0-313-28379-6

HARDCOVER BAR CODE